Our Debt to Greece and Rome

EDITORS

GEORGE DEPUE HADZSITS, PH.D.

DAVID MOORE ROBINSON, PH.D., LL.D.

ROMAN POLITICS

BY
FRANK FROST ABBOTT

COOPER SQUARE PUBLISHERS, INC.
NEW YORK
1963

Published 1963 by Cooper Square Publishers, Inc.
59 Fourth Avenue, New York 3, N. Y.
Library of Congress Catalog Card No. 63-10295

CONTENTS

[v]

CONTENTS

ROMAN POLITICS

ROMAN POLITICS

I. THE ROMAN SYSTEM OF GOVERNMENT

1. PRE-AUGUSTAN

ROMAN political history has an unusual meaning and value for us, because the Romans had to face so many of the problems which confront us today, and their experience ran through such a wide range. Few peoples can boast of an unbroken history of a thousand years, and perhaps none has tried so many different forms of government. The early monarchy gives way to an oligarchy, to be displaced in turn by a democracy. The dual government of the prince and the senate which follows develops into the empire, and the emperor in time becomes the autocratic monarch. In this period of a thousand years from the seventh century before our era to the fourth century after it, we may see in the practical experiences of the

Roman people the points of strength and of weakness in an aristocracy, a plutocracy, a parliamentary government, a democratic empire, and an autocracy. We may also trace in the history of Rome the development of a city-state into a world-wide empire. In its early days the territory of Rome covered scarcely a hundred square miles. Then followed one after another the conquest of Central Italy, of the whole peninsula, of the Western Mediterranean, of the Greek Orient, and of Western Europe and the region of the Danube, until Roman rule extended from the Sahara to the Rhine, from the Tigris and the Euphrates to the Atlantic. This tremendous territorial expansion, which brought within the limits of the State people of diverse races, colors, and religions, called for a constant recasting and readjustment of political forms and methods, and the solution of countless new political problems. In almost all of our colonies or dependencies today, in the Philippines, in Asia, and in Africa we have to deal only with peoples less advanced in civilization than we are, but the Romans had not only to civilize and govern the stubborn tribes of Gaul and Spain, but also to make their authority respected in the Greek East, among peoples who could boast of a civilization far higher and older than their own. That a city-state with the old and narrow local social and political traditions which Rome had could adapt herself to the government of a world-empire composed of such diverse elements as made up the Roman Empire is one of the marvels of history, and a study of the methods which she followed can not fail to throw light on political questions which we have to meet to-day. The range of social and economic conditions through which Rome went is equally wide. The Romans come on the stage of history as a primitive pastoral people with strongholds on the hills. In course of time they build cities all over the world whose beauty and magnificence have perhaps never been equalled. Their government had to keep pace with these social and economic changes, and consequently had to adapt itself to almost every conceivable state of society.

In spite of all these facts one may be inclined to raise the question whether our civilization can have much in common with one so far removed from it in point of time, and whether the study of such an ancient society will have more than an intellectual or historical interest for us. This would be true perhaps if we were studying the political system of almost any other people of antiquity. It is hard for us to understand or sympathize with the social or political ideas of the Egyptians, the Assyrians, or the Persians. Perhaps it is not easy to find much even in the political experiences of the Greeks which will be of practical service to us. But with the Romans it is different. If an immigrant from ancient Rome of the first century before our era should disembark in New York tomorrow, he would need less training in understanding our political machinery than many of our contemporary immigrants do, because the Anglo-Saxon and the Roman show the same characteristics in their political life. Both peoples are opportunists. Both peoples are inclined to meet a new situation by making as little change as possible in the old machinery. Both have a great deal of practical common sense, and no high regard for formal logic or consistency. The Romans had the institution of slavery, and we have developed a complex industrial system through the application of steam and electricity, and steam and electricity have changed the external aspects of our lives. But these differences have not affected deeply the political thinking of the two peoples. We have little in common with any other peoples of antiquity. We have still less with those of the Middle Ages. The ideals of chivalry, of feudalism, of the medieval church, and the submergence of the individual in society, are altogether foreign to our way of thinking. Perhaps it is the incomprehensible nature of these fifteen hundred years of medieval civilization that separate our times from those of the Romans which has prevented us from recognizing our political kinship to the Romans. From this resemblance between Roman civilization and our own, and between the Roman character and our own, it does not necessarily follow that their system of government was closely akin to ours, or that we have inherited many political institutions directly from them. It would, however, naturally mean that many of their political problems would be like ours, and that their method of approaching them would be similar to ours. In some cases they solved these problems with more or less success; in others, they failed. The legacy which they have handed down to us, then, is the practical demonstration in their political life of the merits of certain forms of government and of certain methods of dealing with political and social questions, and the weakness of others. The points of resemblance between the ancient and the modern, and the large extent of our direct and indirect inheritance will be defined later.

The natural political entity in antiquity was the city, with a small outlying territory about it. This state of things the Romans clearly recognized in fixing the status of conquered territory in Italy and across the sea. Thus, after the conquest of Sicily, Rome made her arrangements for ruling the island, not with a government representing all Sicily, but with the sixty-eight individual cities and towns of the island, and the citizens of Syracuse or of Agrigentum derived such rights as they had, not from the fact that they were Sicilians, but from their residence in the one or the other of these two cities.[1] This political system, based on the independent life of a small community, is familiar enough to us in the history of such Italian cities as Venice, Florence, and Siena in the Middle Ages, and preëminently in the story of Geneva under Calvin. In fact the political institution of antiquity which has had the longest life and which has enjoyed an unbroken history up to our own day is that of the city-state. Hundreds of inscriptions from various parts of the world show us the form of government which these municipalities had in Roman times. The control of affairs rested in the hands of an executive, of a small assembly of chosen men, and of the whole body of citizens. The comparative strength of these three elements differed in different cities, and varied from period to period in the history of each city. This was the government which we find in the city of Rome in early days. Continuity was given to it by the senate, or assembly of elders of the resident clans, who, on the death of the king, appointed one of their number to choose the king's successor, whose assumption of office was dependent on the approval of the senate and the people.

Through an aristocratic revolution the kingdom was overthrown, and the king gave place to two annually elected magistrates, called later consuls, who had the right of veto on each other's actions. The consuls were chosen from the ranks of the patricians, or ruling families, and at the end of a year became patricians again. They must therefore have been largely governed in their action by class prejudice. Consequently the position of the classes which lacked political privileges became intolerable. Another element in the situation aggravated the difficulty. Being located in the centre of Italy and on a navigable river, and being far enough from the mouth of the river to be safe from pirates, Rome grew rapidly, and the coming of a large number of immigrants to the city had a profound effect on its political history. The newcomers did not enjoy the same civil and political rights as the members of the original clans, and they were at an economic and social disadvantage.

The constitutional history of Rome for several centuries centres about the struggle of these people and of the other members of the lower classes to remove the limitations which were put on their rights in these four respects. The natural method of guarding the civil rights of the commons against the arbitrary action of the patrician consul was to limit his powers by law. But the Romans did not adopt this method. They chose class repre-

sentatives, called tribunes, who were author-
ized to intervene in person when a plebeian
was being treated unjustly and prevent the
chief magistrate from carrying out his purpose. It is characteristic of the Roman, as
we shall see in other cases, to take this concrete, personal way of bringing about a constitutional reform. The plebeians were at a
disadvantage also, because they were kept
ignorant of legal procedure and could not
maintain their rights before a magistrate.
The details of the law, or the accepted custom,
were known only to the patrician priests and
were handed down by word of mouth from one
generation to another. About the middle of
the fifth century, after a long struggle, this
law was codified and was engraved on twelve
bronze tablets, and the tablets were hung up
in the Forum where they might be read by
any one. These Twelve Tables [2] were regarded by the Romans as the basis of their
civil liberty, and may well be placed by the
side of the Mosaic Code, the laws of Ham-
murabi, the Gortynian Code, and Magna
Charta. As we shall see later, they contained
no formulation of general rights, but stated
clearly and minutely the procedure to be fol-

lowed in civil and criminal actions. If we may accept tradition, both these battles with the patricians were won by the very modern method of Direct Action.

This conquest of civil rights brought the plebeians a larger measure of political rights than they had enjoyed before. It was necessary for them now to organize a popular assembly of their own, in order to elect the tribunes; the tribune became their political leader, and within the next century, under his leadership, the plebeians forced the patricians to admit them to the consulship, and in consequence to the other important magistracies.

In early days the patricians had formed not only a close corporation politically, but also a social caste. Sons of patricians who married plebeian women lost the patriciate, and all the social, political, and religious privileges which went with it. By the Canuleian law in the fifth century the right to intermarry without loss of privileges was guaranteed. Henceforth the state tended to become a unit, and not two separate communities, and in the future when the interests of the two classes were in conflict prominent patricians were often led by kinship to support the plebeian cause at critical moments.

The fourth point about which the struggles in the early period centred was the land question. It was the age-old battle between the great landowner on the one hand and the peasant proprietor, the tenant, and the free laborer on the other. As Rome came into possession of new territory in central Italy by conquest or otherwise, the great landed proprietors managed to get most of it from the state at a nominal rental. The constant wars in which Rome was engaged during her early history called both rich and poor to the front, but the rich man's slaves and dependents kept his land under cultivation, while the peasant's holdings, left without anyone to till them, steadily deteriorated. The peasant found it hard, too, to compete with the great landowner who farmed on a large scale and used slave labor, while the free laborer was crushed in competition with the slave. A solution of these difficulties was sought in the Licinian laws of the fourth century and in later legislation. But this legislation did not reach the root of the trouble, and the land question came up in one form or the other for many generations to plague the Romans. The Licinian laws, perhaps supplemented by later legislation, limited the number of acres of state land to be occupied by an individual, stipulated that interest already paid on debts should be deducted from the principal, and fixed the proportional number of free laborers and slaves to be employed on an estate. The first and second provisions were intended to protect the peasant proprietor and to prevent the growth of large estates at his expense. If these three measures could have accomplished their purpose, that drift from the country to the city which ultimately wrecked the Roman Empire, and which is one of the dangerous tendencies today, might never have taken place.

The rapid growth of Rome and her conquest of adjacent territory not only brought to the surface the economic questions which we have just been discussing, but also necessitated an increase in the number of magistrates to manage the larger population and to meet the more complex conditions which had arisen. In the early Republican period the only important officials with positive powers were the two consuls. They presided over the meetings of the senate and of the assemblies which were made up of the whole people, and they were the chief executives and the judicial and financial officials of the community. They supervised the conquered districts of Italy, represented the city in its dealings with foreign states, and commanded the army. These manifold duties, and in particular the absence of the consuls from the city in carrying on war, made it necessary to relieve them of some of their civil functions. The first step taken in this direction was to increase the importance of a minor police official, the aedile. To this official was assigned the duty of keeping order in public places, of supervising commercial transactions, and later, as a natural development of these two functions, of taking charge of the public games and of providing a supply of grain for the city. The financial duties of the consul were turned over to the censor. First and foremost, of course, among these, were the collection of taxes and the expenditure of public moneys. In order that he might draw up a correct list of taxable property, the censor required every citizen to appear before him every five years and make a statement concerning his property, his business, and the

[15]

main facts of his life. Consequently the censors not only knew the financial status of every Roman, but were also familiar with his occupation and his moral standing in the community. Now the value of a citizen's vote in the principal popular assembly depended on the amount of property which he held, and certain occupations were regarded as beneath the dignity of a senator or likely to interfere with the disinterested performance of his duty. In later times, too, inclusion in the new social order of the knighthood depended on the possession of a certain amount of property. It was natural therefore that the censors, having all the necessary information before them, should assume responsibility for assigning citizens to their proper places in the centuriate assembly, and for revising every five years the lists of senators and knights. This attempt to supervise the morals of the community is one of the most interesting experiments in government which the Romans ever made. It reached certain social evils, like extravagance and cowardice, of which the courts could not readily take cognizance, and the penalties imposed, of loss of voting importance in the assembly or of exclusion from the list of senators or knights, were severe. It may well indicate a gradual growth of wealth in the community and a threatened disappearance of the simple life and the simple virtues of the olden time. What the censors tried to do was to maintain the moral and social standards of earlier days. While the censor's office flourished, deviations from those standards were not defined by law, but were determined by officials, from whose decisions there was no appeal. Perhaps no official in Roman history enjoyed such absolute power within the limits fixed by the penalties which could be imposed.[3] The institution played an important rôle for many decades, but towards the close of the second century before our era, the population had become so large that an examination of the business and the life of every citizen became impossible. One of the objects which the Romans had tried to accomplish by the establishment of the censorship, they attempted later to attain by the passage of sumptuary laws.

The growth of Rome and the consequent increase of public business led the Romans to take his judicial functions from the consul in 367, just as they had previously relieved him of police duties and of financial business. Henceforth a new magistrate, the praetor, took his place in the courts. To no other institution in the Roman political system does the modern world owe so much as it owes to the praetor's office. At first there was only one incumbent of the office, and since his duties confined him to the city he was called the urban praetor. A hundred years later when a second praetor was added, to deal with cases in which one party or both parties to the case were foreigners, the new official was styled the peregrine praetor and in his courts the principles of the law of nations were developed. Sulla ultimately raised the number of praetors to eight. With the institution of the praetor's office our modern court system of judge and jury was firmly established, and a beginning was made in the development of Roman Law. On taking office the praetor published an edict containing the maxims of law and the forms of procedure which would govern him throughout his year of office. This document followed the edict of his predecessor, with such modifications and additions as his own judgment and the needs of the times required. The law in this way became a living thing and constantly adapted itself to the changing needs of society. The later history of the edict and certain additions to the praetor's duties we shall have occasion to notice in another connection.

The increase which the tribune's power underwent during this period almost made his office a new one. With their characteristic hesitation about introducing radical changes in the constitution, and with their tendency to take concrete action, the Romans at the outset had required the tribune to intervene in person when a citizen was being harshly treated. But their common sense showed them in course of time that it was far better to allow the tribune to record his opposition to a bill when it was under consideration than to have him prevent the execution of a law. This change placed a tremendous power in the hands of the tribune in his struggle with the senate and the nobilty.

In the early period the senate had been composed of the representatives of the leading clans, but as public business became more complex, in making out the list of senators the censors gave a preference to ex-magistrates, who were already experienced in public affairs, and in course of time this practice was crystallized into law. The men who thus became senators by virtue of having held the praetorship, or consulship, for instance, were elected to a magistracy, to be sure, by the people, but the prestige of a candidate who could point to magistrates among his ancestors was so great that a " new man " had little or no chance of being elected against him. The results were twofold. A new nobility was established composed of ex-magistrates and their lineal descendants. In the second place the senate, being henceforth made up of men who had had experience in administration at home and abroad, easily gained supremacy both over the magistrates, who held office for a year only, and over the popular assemblies, which were unwieldy and ill-informed on important matters. For a century and a half, down to the time of the Gracchi (i.e., the second century B.C.), this nobility maintained itself, and Rome was ruled by a parliament. This state of things is the more astonishing in view of the fact that at the beginning of this period the democracy had won a complete victory, and the action of the popular assembly was accepted as final on all matters. The anomaly is easily explained by the fact that the senate controlled the magistrates; they only could bring bills before the assemblies, and they dared not submit measures of which the senate disapproved.

The ascendency of the senate during this period was due in no small measure to the necessity of dealing with important foreign affairs, for which the people were not qualified. Between 287 and 133 came the war with Pyrrhus and the acquisition of Southern Italy, the three wars with Carthage and the conquest of the Western Mediterranean, the wars with Macedonia and the subjugation of the Eastern Mediterranean. By 133 Rome's territory included practically all the lands bordering on the Mediterranean. The government of this newly-acquired empire was a peculiarly difficult problem for a city-state. It was somewhat simplified however by the fact that in her ultimate arrangements Rome had to deal with city-states like herself. In Italy, at the outset, she gave conquered cities civil rights and the right of self-government. The Social War in 91–89 B.C. forced her to grant them the political rights of Roman citizens also. Henceforth Italy was a political unit, but, inasmuch as ballots could be cast at Rome only, voters outside the city were at a disadvantage. The Roman Republic never got far enough away from the tradition of the city-state to recognize the fact that citizens could cast their ballots elsewhere than at Rome or that other communities could send their representatives to Rome.

To provide for a new province outside Italy, the senate sent a commission of ten to cooperate with the Roman commander in drawing up a charter. In this document the province was divided into judicial circuits, and the status of each city was fixed either by separate treaty with Rome or by legislative action. Provincial cities were usually permitted to retain their senates, popular assemblies, local magistrates and courts. A few of them were " free cities," exempt from taxation, but most of them were required to pay a fixed sum in taxes, or to turn over to Rome a certain proportion of the annual return from the land. The rate of taxation was not high, but farming out the taxes to contractors, whose sole desire was to extort as much from the provincials as possible, made taxation in the provinces oppressive. Roman governors were often in league with the moneyed interests at Rome, and were themselves anxious to line their pockets during their year abroad. After a period of experimentation the Romans settled down to the practice of sending out ex-consuls and ex-praetors as provincial governors. These men had experience in public affairs, but their term of office was so short that they acquired little knowledge of local conditions and felt little sympathy with the provincials. Public sentiment at Rome could effect no change, because, like most democracies, the Roman democracy felt little interest in the welfare of the provincials.[4]

The tribunates of the two Gracchi [5] at the end of the period which we have been considering begin the century-long revolution which ultimately overthrew the oligarchy and brought in the empire. The attention of Tiberius Gracchus was called to the gradual disappearance of the peasant proprietor from Italy, to the abnormal growth of the city at the expense of the country, and to the crushing out of the middle class. He and his brother set themselves to work to remedy this situation by limiting the size of landed estates, by assigning state lands to home-

steaders, and by drafting off the city's proletariat to colonies in Italy and abroad. In
these plans Tiberius met the violent opposition
of the senate, but carried his measures through
in a popular assembly in spite of the senate's
efforts. By this action, and by securing " the
recall " of a hostile tribune, he struck a fatal
blow at the prestige of the senate, which had
controlled legislation for a century and a half.
Ten years later by securing the passage in the
popular assembly of one bill to supply grain
to the poor of Rome at a price lower than the
market rate, of another imposing a penalty on
a magistrate who carried out the final decree
of the senate suspending certain constitutional
guarantees, and of a third which dealt with
the taxes in Asia, Gaius, the brother of
Tiberius, vindicated the claim of the popular
assembly to be the controlling factor in legislation on domestic and foreign affairs. The
political history of Rome for the next century is a continuation of this life-and-death
struggle between the nobility and the democracy, with one and the other contestant
alternately in the ascendant. The development of the empire and the need of a standing
army to carry on wars abroad and maintain

order, in the end, gave a decisive turn to the struggle.

To maintain its integrity an oligarchy must keep its numbers small and must prevent individuals from gaining too great eminence or popularity. The traditional acceptance by the masses of certain families as the only families qualified to furnish rulers for the state had kept the nobility a close corporation. To accomplish the second object, that is, to prevent an ambitious individual from rising too rapidly to power, from holding his authority too long a time, and from securing too strong and compact a following, the senate had hedged the magistracies about with a number of legal safeguards. The strict laws enacted before the time of the Gracchi against bribery and prescribing a secret ballot were passed to protect the nobility, and not in the interests of morality. Custom at first, and later, legislation, fixed minimum age requirements for most of the offices, established a certain order in which they must be held, and required an interval between the incumbency of two successive magistracies. The reactionary recasting of the constitution under Sulla illustrates well the aristocratic policy in these matters.

In it the important magistracies stand in the order of quaestorship, aedileship, praetorship, and consulship, and a two-year interval was necessary between each two. The minimum age requirement for the consulship was forty-three years, and no one might be reëlected to a magistracy until a period of ten years had expired. This is essentially the system which had been gradually worked out during the flourishing period of the oligarchy. It had also always been a fundamental principle of the Republic that no magistrate should hold office for more than a year, except the censor, whose term was eighteen months. This provision of the constitution took from the magistrate his power and desire to initiate political action. He had been a senator for many years before becoming consul. In twelve months he would be a senator again. He did not lose class-consciousness during his short term of office. If he had wished to assert himself, it would have been impossible. The senate was a body of trained administrators, many of whom had a wider technical knowledge of the questions at issue than he had himself. It was a body of men bound together by mutual self-interest, which had a tradition of centuries behind it. The danger point in the system for the oligarchy lay in the fact that an army and unlimited authority had to be given to the governor of a province. The senate tried to minimize this danger by keeping a tight grip on the purse-strings when appropriating money and in voting troops for the provinces, and by requiring governors to submit their arrangements in the provinces to the senate for ratification, when their terms had expired.

The decline of parliamentarism in the century which lies between the Gracchi and Caesar may be traced in the loss of these safe-guards, one after another. Disorders at home, the pressure of wars abroad and the dominance of the army led to their disregard. A case in point occurred toward the close of the second century before our era. The senatorial leaders had shown great incompetence and venality in their campaigns against the Numidian king Jugurtha, and the popular party forced the election to the consulship of Marius, a man of humble birth, and gave him command of the forces in Africa. His brilliant success in this war made the people turn to him in 104, when the Cimbri and Teutons swept down into Italy and overwhelmed the aristocratic leaders. Once more he succeeded, and was elected to the consulship year after year, until, in the year 100, he held this office for the sixth time. The popularity of Marius brought his son to the consulship before he had reached his twentieth year. Twenty-five years later the senate itself was forced to give up an important feature of its policy. Sertorius, a brilliant democratic leader, had established himself in Spain; he had formed an alliance with Mithridates, Rome's deadly enemy in the East, and threatened to return to Italy and restore the democracy to power. To avert this danger the senate made Pompey proconsul, although he had not yet held even the quaestorship, and sent him to Spain with 40,000 troops. A little later the Gabinian and Manilian laws, carried through by the democracy against the vigorous opposition of the oligarchy, entrusted him with extraordinary powers for a long term to carry on the wars against the Cilician pirates and against Mithridates. The dictatorship of Sulla in 82 B.C. and the sole consulship of Pompey in 52, both of which resulted from disorder in Rome, violated the principle of collegiality which was one of the most important safeguards of the oligarchy. Within one hundred years, then, of the time of the Gracchi all the bulwarks which the aristocracy had built up to protect its position were broken down. " New men " were put in the consulship. Popular favorites attained that office before reaching the minimum age required of candidates, and men were freely reëlected to it. The fixed " order of the offices " and the principle of collegiality were violated.

In its struggle for power, the democracy met a reverse in the suppression of the Catilinarian conspiracy in 63 B.C., so that when Pompey returned from his campaign against Mithridates in the following year, the senate ventured to postone the ratification of his arrangements in Asia and the reward of his veterans. This forced him to make common cause with the democratic leader Caesar, and with Crassus, whose wealth and financial associates made him a man of great influence. In 60 B.C. these three political leaders formed the compact, known as the First Triumvirate, which directed the politics of Rome through its control of the popular assembly for a number of years.[6] Caesar was given the consulship, and later an important command in Gaul. The

death of Crassus in a campaign in Parthia left
Caesar and Pompey face-to-face. Pompey
who had staid in Rome ultimately threw in
his lot with the senatorial party, and, when
in 49 B.C. the senate tried to make Caesar give
up his Gallic province and the Civil War
broke out, Pompey was put in charge of the
army operating against Caesar. Caesar's success in the war made him undisputed master
of Rome, and before his death he became
dictator for life. The liberators, as they called
themselves, made a last stand for the old
régime, but were defeated at Philippi, and the
victors, Octavius, Antony and Lepidus, formed
the Second Triumvirate, the members of which
did not content themselves with the unofficial
position of political bosses, as Caesar, Crassus,
and Pompey had done, but secured a legal
basis for their autocratic power through legislation in the popular assembly. Again the
elimination of one member of the triumvirate,
Lepidus, and the battle of Actium in 31 B.C.
left Octavius, or Augustus as we know him
in later life, in undisputed control of the state.
The revolution was complete. The old machinery of government had broken down under
the strain put upon it by the policy of im-

perialism. Parliamentarism and the narrow policy of a city-state were ill adapted to the government of an empire. The large armies and the long terms of office abroad which Marius and Sulla, Pompey and Caesar had held, had put at their disposal greater resources than the state could command, and the Roman citizens and provincials who had been taught to obey them implicitly in the field maintained their allegiance to their old commanders upon the return of the latter to Italy.

2. Post-Augustan

The problem which confronted Augustus in revising the constitution after the battle of Actium was not simple. He had to provide a just and efficient government for an empire, which included southern and central Europe, the Near East, and northern Africa, without breaking away too violently from the traditions of the city-state. Rome must continue to be the capital. Italy must hold her privileged position above the provinces, and the old organs of government and the old forms and titles must be kept. The political life of the Republic had been embodied in two institutions, the senate and the tribunate. One represented the aristocracy; the other, the aspirations of the democracy. These two organs of government formed the core of the system which Augustus finally adopted. In this arrangement therefore he adhered closely to the tradition of the old city-state.[7] Other considerations reinforced in his mind the argument from tradition. The tribunician power, which he took for life, could be exercised in almost every field of administrative activity. Furthermore, the office was popular, because the tribune had from time immemorial been the champion of the masses and had protected the individual against the encroachments of the state. Probably Augustus also felt that the power of the office, from its nature and history, was capable of indefinite extension in all directions.

Outside of Rome and Italy the problem before him was the improvement of conditions in the provinces.[8] To the provinces also he applied the dual system of control. The supervision of Italy and the management of the older provinces were entrusted to the senate. The border provinces, where troops were stationed, he took into his own hands. He directed the government of them by virtue of the proconsular *imperium* which he held permanently. In this case, as in that of the tribunician power, he held firmly to an old practice, because proconsuls had ruled the provinces for centuries, but he extended the scope of his own *imperium* to cover all the unsettled provinces. This arrangement made him commander-in-chief of all the legions. He also held the power permanently, and he was not required to lay down the *imperium*, as republican proconsuls had done, on entering the city. The whole empire was thus put under the dual control of Augustus and the senate. This is the first instance in history of the establishment of a constitutional monarchy.

The provinces profited greatly by the changes which Augustus made in the method of governing them. The evils of the republican system come out in Cicero's orations against Verres, the governor of Sicily, and in the letters which he wrote while he was himself governor of Cilicia. Governors had been sent out to the provinces without paying much heed to their competence. They received no salary, and their terms were short. The governors whom Augustus sent out were chosen on the score of honesty and fitness. Their terms were long enough to enable them to become familiar with conditions in their provinces. They received a generous fixed salary, and those who were capable and honest might look forward to steady advancement. The older provinces were still under the control of the senate, but the excellence of government in the imperial provinces exercised a beneficial influence upon them also. Italians and provincials welcomed the firm and stable government which the principate of Augustus promised them in the same spirit in which the French accepted Louis Napoleon.

The development of the city-state into a world-empire is well illustrated by the decadence of the popular assembly which represented the narrow, selfish interests of the city of Rome, and we are not surprised to find the election of magistrates transferred from this body to the senate under the successor of Augustus. As for the magistracies they lost their independence in large measure. Augustus introduced the practice of commending certain candidates for office, and his approval assured them election. Consequently they became subordinates in the new executive system, of which he was the head. The functions of government were divided between the prince and the senate, but the lion's share fell to the prince. The senate could not successfully assert, in dealing with him, the claims which it had made good against an annually elected magistrate of much less prestige and power. Another circumstance contributed greatly to lessen the influence of the senate. During his declining years Augustus could not attend all its meetings. Consequently he adopted the practice of sending it his proposals in writing. They were always adopted without change, and propositions of this sort, known as *orationes principis,* became in the course of time part of the law of the land.

The powers which Augustus held were granted to him for life or for a term of years. It was not easy to arrange for their transmission to a successor, but he cleverly surmounted the difficulty by naming Tiberius as heir to his private fortune and by having him invested with the *imperium* and with the tribunician power. The theory of the republican magistracy was kept intact, inasmuch as the two powers just mentioned were conferred on Tiberius by the senate in coöperation with the people, but the action of the popular assembly was a pure matter of form, and the senate could be counted on to approve the choice of the prince. The precedent which Augustus set was followed by his immediate successors.

He materially strengthened his position by clearly marking off certain social classes from the rest of the population and by making their privileges dependent on his favor. No one could become a senator unless he had been elected to a magistracy, and success in an election required the support of the prince. He gave dignity to the knighthood and definiteness to its membership by making important appointments from its ranks, and by revising the list of knights at regular intervals. He even created an aristocracy among the freedmen in the municipalities.

No survey of Roman politics would be complete without some account of political life in these municipalities, for, as we have already noticed, the city was the organic political unit in antiquity. Several municipal charters,[9] most of which have been found within the last fifty or seventy-five years, give us a clear idea of the municipal system in the West and of the efforts which were made in the early empire to improve it and make it uniform. In cities of the typical form there were two local chief magistrates corresponding to the early republican consuls, two minor magistrates who bore the title of aediles, a senate or common council of one hundred members, and a popular assembly. The system adopted was conservative, inasmuch as the control of local affairs rested largely with the local senate, and the magistrates were its ministers. Most cities were allowed to keep a large measure of self-government under the early empire, and this fact kept alive the sentiment of local pride and the local patriotism of the citizens. So long as the cities were free to manage their own affairs, the empire was prosperous. As the cities lost their sense of responsibility, or as the central government encroached on their rights, as it began to do in the second century of our era, the decline of the empire set in. It was to this halcyon period of municipal prosperity from the latter part of the first to the close of the second century that Gibbon pays his famous tribute in the third chapter of his history: "If a man were called to fix the period in the history of the world, during which the condition of the human race was most happy and prosperous, he would, without hesitation, name that which elapsed from the death of Domitian to the accession of Commodus." We need not stop to consider in this connection whether the decline of this prosperity caused the decay of self-government or was due to it. At all events the two processes were contemporaneous.

To return from this brief account of city-life to the story of imperial politics, — as we have noticed, under the system which Augustus set up, there were two recognized sources of authority in the state, the prince and the senate. We say "recognized sources of power," because in the background loomed up the sinister figure of the army, which was still capable of determining the fortunes of the state, as it had done in the times of Sulla and Marius, of Pompey and Caesar. Perhaps we may see the first step toward the intrusion of the army into politics again when Sejanus, the unscrupulous praetorian prefect of Tiberius, brought all the cohorts of the praetorian guard together in Rome. The control of these soldiers stationed in the capital put a powerful weapon in the hands of Sejanus, but, before he could strike, his designs were laid bare.

The hereditary principle which Augustus had introduced, by adopting Tiberius and by conferring imperial honors upon him, a principle which was followed by his immediate successors, was for a time a safeguard for the succession. But when the Julian line became extinct on the murder of Nero, the field lay open to the imperial aspirant who was backed by the strongest army. After a year of struggle between four military leaders, Vespasian made good his claim to the prize, and in the year 69 founded a new dynasty, the Flavian. The precedent which Vespasian had set was not followed for a century, but from the close of the second century to the accession of Diocletian in 284 the praetorian guard and the army constituted the power which made and unmade the rulers of Rome. Within the period of seventy-three years which preceded the reign of Diocletian there were in fact twenty-three different emperors, almost all of whom owed their elevation to the throne to the force of arms, and kept their places on the throne so long as they could keep the favor of their armed supporters.

Vespasian, whose seizure of the imperial purple we noticed a moment ago, was not a native of the city of Rome, as all the members of the Julian line had been, nor did he belong to a noble family. These two facts might almost be taken as an omen of the great change which he and his successors were to bring about in the position of Rome and Italy in the Roman world and in the political standing of the senate. The exceptional position which Rome and Italy had held under the republic was taken from them in part by robbing them of their privileges and in part by raising the provinces to a higher political plane. Augustus had started the new movement by stationing troops in Italy and by taking the municipal departments in Rome under his control. Within a century the same fate befell other Italian municipalities which had befallen Rome, and they had to surrender to the emperor the control of their finances and their jurisdiction in all important civil and criminal cases. The privilege which at first Rome and later the Italian municipalities guarded most jealously was their exclusive right to Roman and Latin citizenship. Claudius turned from this tradition when he granted these privileges to certain Gallic cities, and the Flavian emperors violated it in a still more striking way by their generous treatment of many cities in Spain. The levelling down of Italy to the position of the provinces, so far as citizenship was concerned, was completed when Caracalla in 212 granted Roman citizenship to practically all freemen in the empire.[10] In this connection may be mentioned a significant change which was made in the organization of the army. The legions from the time of Hadrian on were recruited in all parts of the empire, and officers were no longer drawn solely from the Western and Latin-speaking portion of the Roman world, but from the East also. The army therefore ceased to be the great Romanizing influence which it had been in the past, and what was still worse, a feeling of local solidarity grew up which was destined in the end to be fatal to the unity of the empire. It was this feeling which gave rise to the nationalist movement in the third century, and the Gallic kingdom of Postumus in the West in that century and the kingdom of Zenobia in Palmyra in the East were concrete manifestations of this feeling and at the same time premonitions of the future dissolution of the empire.

We noticed not only that Vespasian was

born outside of Rome, but also that he was of lowly birth. Perhaps the latter fact accounts in part for the hostility which the senate showed toward him, and for the effort which it made in the early part of his reign to assert its authority. The movement was short-lived. The prince and the senate were partners of unequal strength in the dyarchy which Augustus had established, and Vespasian soon made this fact clear to the senate. It came out still more clearly in the reign of his younger son Domitian, who had himself made censor for life, and by virtue of this authority drew up the lists of senators to suit his own pleasure. The tradition of the city-state had been violated and the prestige of the senate had been lowered when Julius Caesar admitted provincials to the senate. This revolutionary precedent was freely followed by emperors during the second half of the first century. This transformation of the Roman senate into a body made up of representatives drawn from all parts of the empire was part of the larger change of the Roman *imperium* into an international world-state. The senate was still allowed to elect the emperor, but the election meant nothing more than the formal ratification of a choice made by the candidate's predecessor or by the army, and "Caesar's candidates" for the magistracies were always elected by the senate. The senate's legislative powers had almost disappeared, because the senate had given up to the emperor almost entirely its right of initiative. We have already observed the importance which the "discourses of the prince" had acquired in the field of legislation. Through the opportunity which they gave him of declaring his will, and by the issuance of edicts, decrees and other "constitutions," as they were called, the emperor took the lawgiving power almost completely into his own hands. The one real power which the senate exercised under the empire, long after its legislative and electoral functions had lost most of their meaning, was its right to sit as a court, especially in important political cases. In this capacity it had authority to impose the penalties even of banishment, deportation, and death, but by the beginning of the third century this jurisdiction, except where senators were charged with crimes, had passed to the emperor. By the close of this century the Roman senate had completed the cycle and come back to the status which it had held in the primitive city-state, that of a municipal council.

This gradual loss of power by the senate meant a corresponding increase of course in the influence of the emperor, but his supremacy was assured also by positive additions to his authority in other directions. Hadrian in the early part of the second century built up a bureaucracy [11] so large and so systematically organized that it enabled him and his successors to reach into the remotest parts of the empire and control the government of municipalities and the lives of all the citizens. Probably the world has never known so complete and crushing a paternalistic system as is revealed to us by the *Codes* of Theodosius and Justinian in the fifth and sixth centuries.

The drift toward autocracy was greatly accelerated by the influence which Egypt and the Orient exercised on the development of the principate. Perhaps the Oriental practice of identifying the secular and divine rulers of the world never found complete acceptance in Rome, but the erection of altars in the provinces to Rome and Augustus, the attribution of the titles " Master and God " to

Domitian by his procurators, and in the third century the introduction into the court of Elagabalus of the Persian practice of paying divine honors to the sovereign, the presence of eunuchs in the palace of Aurelian, and the wearing of the Eastern diadem by Diocletian, show clearly enough that the principate was taking on the form of an Oriental despotism. The conception of the emperor's authority which these practices suggest finds expression in the *Code* of Justinian in the sixth century.[12] The first words of the rescript in which Justinian authorizes Tribonian to codify the laws of the empire are: " We, under divine guidance governing our realm, which has been entrusted to us by the powers above, etc." We shall see in the next chapter that under the prevailing theory of Roman lawyers from the second to the sixth century the emperor derived his authority from the people, but this utterance of Justinian and other passages in the *Code* show us the beginnings of the doctrine of the divine right of kings which Rome transmitted from the Orient to the states of modern times. When this point in the development of the empire had been reached, the preëminence of the city of Rome had gone, the distinction between Italy and the provinces had been obliterated, Roman citizenship had lost its significance, the splendor of the senate and the magistracies had faded, and the municipalities, which had been the pride and glory of the early empire, were plunged in poverty and wretchedness. In their place is an autocrat, kept in power by an army made up largely of barbarians, who carried out his wishes through a bureaucracy; and this, in turn, was supported by a body of citizens divided into groups by a system of castes, and held in most cases to the soil and to their hereditary occupations by the will of the state.

II. ROMAN POLITICS AND MODERN POLITICS

1. ROME AND THE CHURCH OF ROME

IN THE brilliant argument which Belloc makes in *Europe and the Faith* to prove that " the Roman Empire with its institutions and its spirit was the sole origin of European civilization," he goes so far as to maintain that " the divisions and subdivisions of Europe, the parish, the county, the province, the fixed national traditions with their boundaries, the routes of communication between them . . . all these derive entirely from the old Roman Empire, our well-spring." He finds in the Church of Rome the medium through which this inheritance has been transmitted. With this Catholic essayist the Protestant historian, Harnack, is in substantial agreement when he writes: " The Empire has not perished, but has only undergone a transformation. . . . The Roman Church is the old Roman Empire consecrated by the Gospel."

Before we take up for consideration certain points of resemblance and of difference between our political institutions and those of ancient Rome, it is interesting to stop for a moment to ask ourselves in what respects the tradition and the ideals of the Roman state have been perpetuated by the Church of Rome. In the first place the Church is the lineal successor of the Empire in the sense that she saved Europe from chaos when the political ties which bound its several component parts to Rome were severed, and she conserved with all her power through the Middle Ages the Roman elements which escaped being engulfed by the wave of barbarism. More than that, she kept alive the old tradition of world-empire, no longer of the flesh, but of the spirit. Like the old Empire her domain embraced diverse lands and peoples. She resembled and she resembles the Empire now in the fact that she follows law and tradition strictly. She requires implicit obedience from the individual, and the interests of the individual are subordinated to those of the organization. In all these characteristics she is the true spiritual daughter of the Roman Empire. We noticed a moment ago that the realm of the Church,

[48]

like that of the Emperor, included many
different lands. The territorial parallelism between the two systems goes beyond this general point of resemblance.

As Sohm has put it in his *Outlines of Church
History,* " the city or *civitas* was the lowest
political unit of the Empire. It became the
lowest political unit of the Church. In the
constitution of the Church the territory of the
city appeared as the episcopal diocese. In
the constitution of the Empire the province,
with the provincial governor, stood above the
civitas. The episcopal dioceses were united in
like manner under the direction of the metropolitan, the bishop of a provincial capital,
forming an ecclesiastical province. In the
constitution of the Empire, from the fourth
century, several provinces composed an imperial diocese under an imperial governor
(*vicarius*). The imperial diocese also (at
least in certain parts of the Eastern Greek
Church) formed, after the fourth century, part
of the ecclesiastical constitution, as the dis-
trict of a patriarch, to whom the metropolitans
of the imperial dioceses were subordinate.
Finally the general union of the churches
corresponded to the general union of the

[49]

Empire, with the imperial Council (the so-called Oecumenical Council) as its legitimate organ. . . . Thus in its old age the Roman Empire bequeathed its constitution to the young Church. . . . It was its last great legacy to the future."

And later Sohm goes on to say: " To this day the diocese of the Catholic bishop is the copy of the Roman *civitas;* the province of the Catholic archbishop, the copy of the Roman imperial province; and the Catholic Church under a Pope declared omnipotent by law, the copy of the ancient Roman Empire, with its Caesars who claimed the world as their possession." The Church extended its limits in ancient times and still extends them by new conquests, just as the Empire did. The missionary expeditions of Gregory in the sixth century, like the Jesuit enterprises in North and South America in recent times, were carried out in the spirit of Caesar or Trajan, and, after the Christian conquest of England, Gregory spoke as a Roman Emperor might have spoken, when he said " In one faith He linked the boundaries of the East and the West." The absolute power of the Emperor in the later period is continued in tradition by the infallibility of the Pope, and the remarks of the city prefect, Themistius, to Theodosius the Great, "thou art the living law," might be made with propriety to the Pope of today. The title "Pontifex Maximus" is common to both rulers, and there is a striking similarity between other ecclesiastical titles and those in the official Roman list of the *Notitia Dignitatum*. Latin is the official language of the Church, as it was of the Empire; the Pope consults the College of Cardinals, as the Emperor consulted the Senate; Canon Law, which has been derived in part from Roman Civil law, is codified as Roman Law was; the Councils seem to follow the parliamentary procedure of the Roman Senate, and the dress of Church officials is reminiscent of Roman times. In other words, what is characteristic of the spirit of the organization and of the externals of the Church of Rome is a direct inheritance from the Empire.

2. THE INDIVIDUAL AND THE STATE

Let us pass now to consider the relation which our political theories and institutions bear to those of Rome. A wise government aims to strike a judicious balance between the rights of the individual and the safety and welfare of the community. This happy mean can best be determined by watching the play of the two principles in concrete cases. Such an opportunity is offered to us by the history of the ancient city-state which sets before us examples in which the two ideals of government mentioned above are combined in varying degrees. These instances range from Athens which favored the freedom of the citizen to Delphi or Sparta which exalted the importance of the commonwealth.

We owe also to the Greeks and Romans the discussion of another fundamental political problem and various attempts to solve it. Is the ideal state a state ruled by one person, by a few persons, or by all the citizens? This question was discussed with great acumen and learning by Greek writers on political theory, and their views with certain modifications have been transmitted to us by Cicero in his treatise *On the Commonwealth*. Indeed the merits and defects of all systems of government have been exemplified in the history of Rome itself,

which ran through the entire gamut of governmental forms.

The two most important Roman writers of
the classical period on political theory were
Cicero and Seneca. Unfortunately only a part
of Cicero's treatise *On the Laws* has come
down to us, and only fragments of his book
On the Commonwealth are extant, but these
two works were known in their entirety to the
early Roman jurists and to the Christian
Fathers, and have exerted a great influence on
them, and through them, upon us. Even in
their present fragmentary form they show us
what an important contribution Cicero has
made to political philosophy. Quite outside
the fact that he served as an intermediary between Greek political thinking and that of our
own times, his two works are of great value
to us, both because of Cicero's method of approaching the subject of the state and because
of his conception of the organization of society.
Most of Cicero's predecessors, with the exception of Panaetius and Polybius, direct their
attention to the ideal state, to an imaginary
commonwealth. Cicero in his *Commonwealth,
De Re Publica*, II. 1. 3, tells us that it is his
purpose to study the Roman state " in its birth,

its growth, its maturity, and in its present strength and vigor." In other words he introduces the modern method of studying the organization of actual states, and we have set forth, perhaps for the first time, the fruitful conception of the state as an organism.

In discussing the organization of society, Cicero finds the source of law and justice, not in utility, but in nature. Right and wrong are determined *naturae norma*, (*De Legibus*, I. 16. 44). This law of nature is not one thing in Rome, another in Athens; it is not one thing today, another tomorrow, but it is eternal and immutable, (*De Re Publica*, III. 22. 33). This conception of the *ius naturale* was taken up by Ulpian in the third century and by other early jurists, developed in the *Code* of Justinian, and handed down through the Middle Ages to our own time. It covers " that body of principles of justice and reason which men can rationally apprehend, and which forms the ideal norm or standard of right conduct and of the justice of social institutions." From the Civil law it passed into Canon law through the encyclopedic work of St. Isidore in the seventh century, and gave rise to the tripartite division which Gratian sets forth in the *Decretals,*

when he writes: "*Ius naturale* appears with
the beginnings of the rational creation, and
remains unchangeable: the *ius consuetudinis*
(i.e., the *ius gentium*) had its inception later,
when men began to live together. . . . But the
ius constitutionis (i.e., the *ius civile*) begins
with the principles which the Lord delivered
to Moses," i.e., with written law.   These dis-
tinctions have furnished the starting point in
most modern discussions of the subject.
Cicero defined the Commonwealth as "the
affair of the people, but the people is not any
assemblage of men, gathered together in any
fashion, but a gathering united under a common law and in the enjoyment of a common
well being," (*De Re Publica*, I. 25. 39).   From
this definition he seems to imply that the state
has a twofold purpose, to protect the individual, and to promote his welfare.   In one
passage in his *Commonwealth*, (*De Re Publica*,
III. 13. 23), he makes a speaker in the dia-
logue enunciate a theory of the state, out of
which Rousseau may well have developed his
doctrine of the Social Contract: "But when
one person fears another, when man fears man,
and class, class, then, since no one trusts his
own strength, a compact is made between the

[55]

people and the rulers, out of which springs that which Scipio approved — a state whose form is determined by agreement." This theory of the Social Compact, probably derived from Cicero, was put forth again in the eleventh century. So far as the form of the state goes, it may be monarchical, aristocratic, or democratic, or these three elements may be combined in it, as Cicero thought they were in the Roman state; Cicero followed Aristotle and particularly Polybius, in the latter's discussion of the constitutions of Rome and Sparta. The views which Cicero held on this point were taken up for consideration and emphatically denied by Jean Bodin in his great work on the state in the sixteenth century.

Cicero regards any government as legitimate which secures justice and promotes the well being of all its citizens, but he is dissatified with monarchy or aristocracy. As the Carlyles have remarked, in their *History of Mediaeval Political Theory in the West,* which has been of great service to me at many points in this chapter in tracing the development of Roman political doctrines through the Middle Ages, Cicero believed that " every citizen had in him some capacity for political authority, some capacity which ought to find a means of expression." Another fundamental social conception which comes to the surface in Cicero, and is still more clearly stated in Seneca and Marcus Aurelius and the Christian writers, is that of the homogeneity of the human race, the brotherhood of man. To the Greeks, before the time of Stoicism, there was a great gulf between themselves and the barbarians. The Romans showed sometimes a similiar contempt for other people, but they recognized the intellectual and artistic superiority of the Greeks. A century and a half before Cicero's time Plautus seriously or humorously refers to his countrymen as barbarians, when compared with the Greeks. In other words the Romans believed in their own superiority in some fields of human activity, but recognized their inferiority to other peoples in other respects. This made them tolerant of the institutions and practices of races which were brought within the Empire, and formed the basis of that conception of the brotherhood of man which did so much to ameliorate the condition of the lowly, and which is the ideal towards which we somewhat ineffectually strive today. Allied to this cosmopolitan doctrine of the brotherhood of man, was the Roman doctrine concerning the composition of individual societies or states. Aristotle's theory of the organization of society presupposes the inequality of the men who compose it. Cicero believed in natural equality. We are alike, he says, in esteeming the same virtues, in hating the same vices, in our possession of reason and in our capacity for acquiring knowledge. Seneca is almost at the point of extending this conception of natural equality to include even slaves, for, as he says in his treatise on *The Giving and Receiving of Favors:* "fortune has granted the slave's body to his master, he buys it and sells it, but the soul of a slave can not be bought and sold." We shall have occasion to return to this point later, but, while we are speaking of Seneca, it may be well to mention his explanation of the origin of the law of nature which was discussed a few moments ago. The existence of the *ius naturale* presupposes a state of nature antecedent to the conventional institutions of society. This golden age was not one of perfection, but rather of innocence. Avarice brought it to an end. The institutions of society were made necessary by the weaknesses of human nature. This view of Seneca harmonized with the conception which the Christian Fathers later held of the condition of man before the Fall, before sin came into the world, and has been transmitted by them to us.

To return now to the doctrine of the natural equality of men and to the belief that the universal capacity for the exercise of political authority should find adequate expression, out of these principles grew the doctrine which Roman lawyers from the second to the sixth century have noted here and there in the *Codes,* that the power which a government exercises is derived from the people. This source of authority the emperors recognized in the *Codes* up to the time of Justinian. As the Carlyles have shown, this doctrine was accepted by the lawyers in the Middle Ages. It applies to judicial authority, as Bulgarus of Bologna teaches in the twelfth century, and to legislative power, as Irnerius of the same century holds. Their arguments come from the Roman period, because they are drawn from the *Corpus Iuris Civilis,* and they borrow phrases from the *Digest* and the *Code.* The question naturally arose in their minds whether the people could resume their authority or not. Scholars were divided on this point. Some of them maintained that the popular will still found expression in custom, and that therefore custom could override law. Most of them believed that universal custom had this power, but that local custom did not. Consequently they held that the sovereignty of the people still found expression in custom. In passing we may note that we have here the distinction between " unwritten " and " written " law or between common law and statute law. The theory that the authority in the state emanated from the people continued to be the prevailing doctrine as late as the middle of the thirteenth century, as the Carlyles have shown. It is maintained by Nicholas of Cues in the fifteenth century. In his *Systematic Politics, Confirmed by Examples from Sacred and Profane History,* published in 1610, the Calvinist, Johannes Althusius, carried the doctrine to its logical conclusion that, since the authority in a state rested on a contract between the people and their ruler, the people had the right to depose him and resume their delegated power. Hobbes in his *Leviathan,* which appeared in 1641, believed in the principle of the contract, but in his opinion the compact is made by the members of society with one another. The ruler does not enter into the covenant. Consequently he is not bound by it. The radical teachings of Althusius lay dormant for a century and a half, to be taken up by Rousseau in his *Contrat Social* and to form the basis of the famous " Declaration of the Rights of Man " of 1789.

As Pollock has put it in his *Introduction to the History of the Science of Politics:* According to Rousseau " every man gives up himself and his individual rights as fully as in Hobbes' covenant. But the surrender is to the whole society, not to a sovereign. The government is not the sovereign, but a mediator between the community in its corporate capacity and its individual members as subjects." In his *History of the Theory of Sovereignty since Rousseau,* Merriam has traced the development of the doctrine into our own times. The conclusion at which he arrives for our own day is that " those who adhere to the sovereignty of the general will or of public opinion, sentiment, reason, do not mean that this sovereign is at any given moment organized to express the will of the State; they mean that it is to

[61]

be obeyed, not immediately but ultimately."
Modern theory therefore has come back to the
position of Cicero and the Roman jurists,
although, as Bryce has said in his *Modern
Democracies,* the acceptance and development
of the doctrine of popular sovereignty by
Rome, "was due to the pressure of actual
grievances far more than to any theories re-
garding the nature of government and the
claims of the people." Before leaving the
subject of popular sovereignty it is worth while
noticing the limitations under which it is
exercised even in a pure democracy and the
transformation which a democracy inevitably
undergoes. On the first point, if we recall the
history of the Roman Republic which has been
sketched in the preceding chapter, we shall
feel that, although Bryce is speaking of
modern democracies, no more accurate description can be given of the limitations which
hemmed in the Roman democracy than is to
be found in his statement that "popular powers
are in practice more frequently negative or
deterrent than positive. The people can more
readily reject a course proposed to them than
themselves suggest a better course." Equally
applicable to the history of the patriciate, the

senatorial oligarchy, and the plutocracy under the Republic is his remark, drawn from a study of modern conditions, that "nature is always tending to throw power into the hands of the Few, and the Few always tend by a like natural process to solidify into a Class, as the vapours rising from the earth gather into clouds. Fortunately the Class, by a like process, is always tending to dissolve. . . . Thus Free Government cannot but be, and has in reality always been, an Oligarchy within a Democracy."

The opposite doctrine to the one which we have been considering, that of the divine right of kings, comes to the surface sporadically in the *Code* of Justinian, but it is not definitely formulated until we reach the time of Gregory the Great in the sixth century. He develops the new doctrine fully in his *Pastoral Rules* and in his treatise on the book of Job, as the Carlyles have shown, and it is from him that it passed down into the Middle Ages and into later times. The Carlyles trace its development to three causes: (1) the need of checking the anarchical tendency of the primitive Church; (2) the favored position which the Church had under the protection of the Em-

peror after the conversion of Constantine; and
(3) the influence of the Old Testament conception of the position of the King of Israel.
The teachings of the Old Testament were reinforced by those of the New Testament. In
the *Epistle to the Romans* we read, for instance: " Let every soul be subject unto the
higher powers. For there is no power but of
God; the powers that be are ordained of God,"
and elsewhere: " Submit yourselves to every
ordinance of man for the Lord's sake; whether
it be to the king, as supreme; or unto
governors, as unto them that are sent by him
for the punishment of evil doers, and for the
praise of them that do well," I. *Peter*, ii.
13–14. This second explanation of the source
of authority in the state, which the phrases
used by the Roman jurists occasionally suggest, was accepted by the early Church and
transmitted by it through the Middle Ages to
modern times. The king was answerable only
to God. To resist him was impious.

A modification of the theory of the divine
right of kings comes in as the influence of the
Papacy increases. Dante in his work *On
Monarchy* has stated the situation clearly,
when he writes: " Therefore man had need

of two guides for his life, as he had a twofold
end in life; whereof one is the Supreme
Pontiff, to lead mankind to eternal life, according to the things revealed to us; and the other
is the Emperor, to guide mankind to happiness
in the world, in accordance with the teaching
of philosophy." But unfortunately these two
fields of activity overlapped each other, and it
was not easy to say what the theoretical and
practical relation of these two supreme powers
to each other was. Pope Leo III had placed
the crown on the head of Charlemagne in
Rome in the year 800. What the Pope had
given in the name of the people of the Roman
world, he could take away, and at the death
of an emperor, the control of the empire returned to the hands of the Pope. The great
Pope, Hildebrand, in the eleventh century held
firmly to this theory. As the Carlyles have
pointed out, he had a search made in the papal
archives and found what he believed to be
convincing evidence of the feudal dependence
of the different kingdoms of Europe on the
Roman See. In the next century the great
English scholar John of Salisbury writes in his
Policraticus: " the sword, the symbol of
worldly power, the prince receives from the

[65]

hand of the Church." Feudalism inculcated the idea that each man owed allegiance to some one above him, the vassal to his lord, the lord to the prince, the prince to the Emperor, and it was only natural to complete the system by deriving the power of the Emperor from the Pope, whose responsibility was to God. This conception of the Pope as the ultimate source of authority throughout the world with his seat in Rome continued the tradition of the unity of the Roman Empire, which, as we shall soon see, was one of the most potent influences at work throughout the Middle Ages. The history of medieval political theory and practical politics in the Middle Ages turns largely upon the conflict of these two doctrines, that the secular ruler received his authority from the people or directly from God, or that it came to him from the Pope, the vicegerent of God.

Bryce's dictum that " every Monarchy becomes in practice an Oligarchy " sums up the story of the Roman Empire. The Emperor could not in person attend to all the business of the state. He had to organize the government in departments, and delegate authority to the men whom he put at the head of these departments. This was the plan, which, as we noticed, Hadrian brought to completion in the organization of his bureaucratic system, and we are not surprised to find in the *Codes* of Theodosius and Justinian abundant evidence of the unrestrained power which this oligarchy exercised. Both the monarchies and the democracies of today are adopting the Roman plan in the one form or the other. In Germany and in certain other Continental countries before the World War a highly organized bureaucratic system had been developed, while in the United States we have temporary or permanent Federal commissions and boards, like the Interstate Commerce Commission, the Coal Commission, and the Railroad Labor Board, and many of the States have public service commissions. All these have been added in late years to the traditional bureaux and departments. " Government by commission " has become a political catch-word, in some of our electoral campaigns, and some of our political leaders fear that the intrusion of the Federal or State government into the matters of everyday life and into local affairs will restrain individual initiative and undermine the integrity of local government. This

result, at least, followed the development of
the paternal and bureaucratic system of Rome.

3. ON CONSTITUTIONS

While it cannot be said that the constitutional development of England and of countries whose constitutions are like hers can be
traced in all respects to Rome, it may be said
with truth that the growth and character of
their constitutions bear a strong resemblance
to those of Rome, and that writers and political leaders, especially from the time of the
French Revolution to our own day, have
studied Roman political institutions and have
applied the lessons drawn from their study to
the political and constitutional questions of
the day. In Rome under the Republic the
people when they expressed their wish in the
assembly were omnipotent, just as the decision
of the English people voiced in Parliament is
final. As it is in England, so in Rome the
latest pronouncement of the popular will
rendered null and void any previous enactment
or statute in conflict with it. Rome had no
formal written constitution any more than
England has, but as in England such legal

documents as Magna Charta, the Habeas Corpus Act, and the Parliament Act of 1911 are recognised as being more fundamental than the ordinary statute, so in Rome under the Republic the Laws of the Twelve Tables, the enactment that a citizen charged with a capital offence had the right of appealing to the people, and the principle that a *lex*, or action of the popular assembly, took precedence of a decree of the senate, were so embedded in tradition that no measure could be passed in violation of the principles underlying them. Under the Empire, however, we find a document which, so far as it goes, resembles somewhat a written constitution, viz, the "Law of Vespasian conferring the imperium." [13] In this document we have a comprehensive and systematic recital of the fundamental rights, powers, and privileges of the Emperor. As we have just seen, Rome and England have not defined the functions of the several organs of the state and their relation to one another in a single document, with which all statutes, judicial decisions, and administrative acts must conform, to be valid, as the United States, France, Switzerland and most other modern nations have done. How-

[69]

ever, the laws, precedents, and customs which
direct the public life of England and directed
that of Rome in a sense make up their constitutions. Constitutions of this sort, as Bryce
maintains in his *Studies in History and Juris-
prudence,* are flexible. They bend but do not
break under the temporary blasts of popular
passion or emotion. They have grown up
with the people and are part of the fibre of
the people. Going back, as they do, into the
past, they have the mystery and the dignity
which antiquity gives them. The character
of the Roman and of the English constitutions
reflect the character of the two peoples and
their likeness to each other. They bring out
the practical qualities of the two nations, their
respect for the past, and their ability to adapt
their institutions to new conditions. One more
point of similarity between Roman and Anglo-
Saxon fundamental laws lies in the fact that
both are concrete, and concern themselves
little with political doctrines. Both peoples
drove straight at specific abuses, without
citing any principles of abstract right in justi-
fication of the proposed reform.

In one respect Roman government differed
fundamentally from that of most modern

states. The three functions of government which Montesquieu clearly recognized, the executive, legislative, and judicial, were not assigned to three different classes of officials with as much care as they are today. Of course this lack of differentiation is more noticeable in the early period than it is in the later, but it persists even into the Empire. The Senate, for instance, under the Empire not only legislated, but it nominally had the right to elect the Emperor and the magistrates, and also sat as a court to hear political charges made against members of the senatorial order. Although the threefold division of governmental powers was observed then only in part in the actual organization of the Roman state, it was recognized by Aristotle and by Cicero in their works on politics. The Greco-Roman doctrine on this subject was reaffirmed by Bodin and Locke, as Garner has pointed out in his *Introduction to Political Science,* before it was set forth as a fundamental principle of political organization in the *Spirit of the Laws.* The teachings of Montesquieu on this point became a part of the political philosophy of the French Revolution. In England Blackstone maintained, as Montesquieu had done, that there could be no public liberty when the right of making and enforcing the law was vested in the same man or the same body of men, or when the judicial power was not separated from the legislative and executive. The makers of the Constitution of the United States were profoundly influenced by Montesquieu and Blackstone, and probably no modern constitution exemplifies so well as does the American constitution the threefold division of powers recognized by Cicero. As the Supreme Court has said in one of its decisions: " It is believed to be one of the chief merits of the American system of written constitutional law that all powers entrusted to the government, whether state or national, are divided into three grand departments, the executive, the legislative and the judicial; that the functions appropriate to each of these branches of government shall be vested in a separate body of public servants, and that the perfection of the system requires that the lines which separate and divide these departments shall be broadly and clearly defined."

If we should try to set down the valuable contributions which the Romans have made to modern political theory, or the achievements of the Romans which we may study with profit, or the political qualities in them which we may imitate to advantage, or the important political principles or institutions which we have inherited from them, we should think of the doctrines of popular sovereignty, of the equality and brotherhood of man, of the practical proof which they have given us of the value of a flexible constitution, of their teachings concerning the theory of the state, and of their introduction of the historical method of studying political institutions. Of all these contributions to modern civilization we have already spoken. We should also think of their devotion to the state, of their regard for law and tradition, of their wise opportunism which made their political thinking practical and concrete, of their development of a marvellous body of civil law, of their careful observance of the principle of local self-government, with its acceptance of local institutions and practices, and of their success in promoting law and order and a feeling of social solidarity, in improving material conditions throughout the world, and in governing and civilizing backward peoples. This is a long list, but in all these respects

the political acumen of the Romans was noteworthy, and their achievements either lie at
the basis of modern civilization, as we shall
see, or may furnish us guidance in our political development. In our discussion of the
different branches of the government, and of
various fields of political activity, we shall
have occasion to take up in detail many of
these points which have not yet been
mentioned.

4. THE LEGISLATIVE AND EXECUTIVE BRANCHES OF GOVERMENT

i. RESEMBLANCES BETWEEN ANCIENT AND MODERN

It may be convenient at the outset to com-
pare some of the characteristics of the legislative branch of the Roman government with
those of modern parliaments. The Roman
method of legislating was very similar in
its essential features to that followed by the
states of this Union which freely use the initiative and referendum.[14] These two political devices come to us of course from
Switzerland. One or both of them in their
present form may be traced to Rousseau's

opposition to representative government and to his advocacy of the doctrine of popular sovereignty. But traces of the referendum may be found in certain Swiss cities long before Rousseau's day, and the legislative principle which underlies it may possibly be an inheritance from Roman times, preserved through the Middle Ages in the independent Italian cities. Where the referendum prevails, an elected assembly, the Legislature in our states and the Greater Council in the Swiss cantons, is set over against the whole body of citizens, voting in this country in their home towns, or in Switzerland at some central point. Either legislative organization may initiate legislation, and in practice most proposals originate in the elected body, from which important or controversial matters are referred to the people. Popular action overrides that of the chosen body. The people may not amend a proposal, but must vote " Yes " or " No " upon it. This is an exact description of the relation of the Roman senate to the popular assembly under the Republic. The ancient system had the merits and defects which we see in its modern counterpart. The assembly of the people helped to preserve the

rights of the democracy and gave expression
to popular aspirations. The aristocratic body,
being made up of experienced politicians and
administrative officials, was better qualified to
deal with technical questions and foreign affairs, and the relative importance of the two
legislative organizations varied from one period to another according to the predominance
of the one set of questions or the other.
Naturally the problems arising out of long-
continued wars increased the prestige of the
Roman Senate, just as its exclusive right to
approve treaties of peace with the Central
European States has enhanced the authority
of the American Senate at the expense of the
Lower House. We noticed above that a few
important matters were reserved to the Roman
popular assembly. One of these was the declaration of an offensive war. Now in the
last two or three years in casting about for
some means to avert future wars, it has been
proposed to take the right of declaring war
from the Congress and to submit the question
in each case to the people. This proposal
has been made partly in the belief that the
people who must bear the brunt of a war will
lean toward peace. If we may draw an infer-

ence from the attitude of the Roman people, this conclusion is unfounded. Professor Tenney Frank in his *Roman Imperialism* has shown that the great war with Pyrrhus, the First Punic War, and perhaps the Jugurthine War were forced on Rome by the democracy against the desire and the judgment of the Senate. The Senate knew better than the people what sacrifices of blood and treasure such wars would mean.[15]

In one of the chapters of his book on *Society and Politics in Ancient Rome* the present writer has attempted a comparison between the Roman Senate and the Senate of the United States.[16] The Roman Senate was, and our Senate is, engaged in a struggle with the executive and with another legislative body more popular than itself for the control of the state. The life terms of Roman senators and the comparatively long terms of our own senators put them largely beyond the reach of popular sentiment, and give them a feeling of security in their positions. The long and honorable tradition of both bodies and their *esprit de corps* strengthen this sense of security. Roman senators showed for one another the same senatorial courtesy which has become a byword with us. An element of strength in both organizations is the absence, as a rule, of clôture. A measure submitted by an executive may easily be talked to death or amended so as to bear slight resemblance to the original proposal, if there is little or no limitation on debate. But two powers in particular, enjoyed by both bodies, would give any legislative organization an excellent means of controlling public policy and of directing the administration of public affairs. I mean the right to confirm important appointments and to be consulted in the settlement of foreign affairs. What a tremendous influence the Senate of the United States can exert through its right to participate in the management of foreign affairs we have seen illustrated within the last few years, and, as we have noticed in Chapter I, the Roman Senate held the same position of advantage. Just as our senators control in large measure the appointment to important offices, so the Roman Senate rewarded with lucrative posts in the provinces the politicians who supported its policies, and punished leaders like Caesar who opposed it, with provinces " of forests and marshes." It may be added also that, as has been observed in Chapter I, the Roman Senate was made up of former administrative officials who were familiar from past experience with the questions which came before it, and the Romans did not have the two-party system, which strengthens the hands of a government in Anglo-Saxon countries. It is not strange, therefore, that in course of time the Roman Senate reduced the magistrate to the position of its minister, and that its policy became his policy. As in most modern countries, the members of the government attended the meetings of the legislative body and voted in it. It is interesting to bear the fact in mind that we have felt in the United States the unfortunate results which arise in the making of laws from the lack of close coöperation between the legislative and executive branches of our government, and it has been proposed lately to adopt the Roman practice to the extent of allowing members of the Cabinet to attend meetings of the Congress, without giving them the right to vote.

ii. DIFFERENCES BETWEEN ANCIENT AND MODERN

We have been speaking of points of resemblance between the Roman Senate and the Senate of the United States. Some striking points of difference between its procedure and that of modern legislative chambers should be mentioned. A member of our Senate or House of Representatives, if he were summoned to a meeting of the Roman Senate, would be as astonished at the lack of parliamentary machinery, as was the Connecticut Yankee of Mark Twain's story at the lack of labor-saving devices in the court of King Arthur. He would find no fixed order of business, no quorum ordinarily required, no committees to collect facts and make recommendations, motions not put in writing, and no minutes kept. He would be still more astounded to find three or four mutually exclusive motions before the house at the same time, from which the presiding officer was allowed to make his choice. Yet no legislative body has left behind it such a marvellous record of business-like achievement as the Roman Senate has. This fact may well lead us to ask the question whether the elaborate procedure and the complicated parliamentary rules which our legislative bodies follow are necessary for the expeditious transaction of business. This is not to say that the Roman method could be adopted out of hand today. That was a matter of growth, but it may at least suggest that it would be possible and wise for us to simplify our procedure. Many of the practices peculiar to the Roman Senate may be explained out of its history. Although it is the most famous legislative body known, in theory it was not a legislative body at all. It was in its origin only the Advisory Council, or *consilium,* of the chief magistrate. Its members were merely the experienced old men whose advice the king, and later the consul, sought. When he needed counsel he called them together, and asked their opinions, following naturally the order of age and eminence. In its outward forms the circumstances of its origin were never forgotten. The Senate never met unless the magistrate called it together. The business of the day was laid before it by the presiding officer. Its members were not expected to give their opinions until he asked them, and the presiding officer who was asking

[81]

advice could naturally pick out the proposal which seemed to him wisest and ask the judgment on it of the other members, and it was the traditional practice to make these proposals orally.

Up to the time of Tiberius Gracchus, near the close of the second century before Christ, Rome was under a parliamentary government, not unlike the government of France or Italy in its essential characteristics. Under the constitution of 1875, for instance, the chief executive of France is brought under the control of the legislative body, just as the Roman Consul was made subject to the Senate. All his acts of every kind, to be valid, must be countersigned by one of his ministers, and it is always within the power of the Chamber of Deputies to overthrow a ministry. In the absence of the two-party system in Rome, and the consequent lack of a compact party organization to support the Government, the Roman system was also like that which is common on the Continent. Of course the Roman system was pure parliamentary government in a higher degree than is the system in vogue in any modern state, because the internal and external policy of Rome was not thought of as the policy of Catulus or Messalla, but as that of the Senate, whereas today, with a certain measure of propriety, we speak of the policy of a Briand or of a Giolitti.

Of course the most marked difference between the Roman Senate and modern legislative bodies lies in the fact that in the composition of the ancient body the representative principle was not recognized. It seems to us extraordinary that when, in her early career, Rome absorbed neighboring Latin towns, and when, at the conclusion of the Social War, she gave Roman citizenship to the cities of Italy, she did not authorize them to elect representatives to the Senate. Instead of doing so she required the people of these places to come to the city of Rome, if they wished to vote. In view of this fact it is often said that the Romans were not familiar with the representative system.[17] This conclusion is, however, incorrect. Traces of the system may be found among the Latins in the earliest times, in the sending of delegates from the several towns to the Latin Games. Twice later in the fifth and third centuries B.C., it was proposed in the Senate to allow Latins to elect a certain number of the members to that body. The constitution which the Italic State adopted in the Social War seems to have been based on the representative idea, and the system which Aemilius Paullus introduced into Macedonia in 168 B.C. was apparently a unicameral, representative government. The Romans then were not ignorant of the principle of representative government, but they did not adopt the system for Italy and the empire because, by doing so, Rome would have lost her exclusive rights, the balance of power would have passed from the Latins, and in course of time provincial members of the Senate would have outnumbered even the Italians. The lack of elected provincial representatives in the Senate was made up in some measure under the empire by the readiness which the emperor showed to listen to the requests and complaints of individuals and cities all over the world, and by the establishment of provincial assemblies, called Κοινά in the East and *concilia* in the West. When the Romans acquired Greece and Asia they found that neighboring cities in these two regions had already formed religious organizations or political federations. One of these organizations, the assembly of Asia, toward the close of the first century B.C. asked permission to establish the cult of Rome and Augustus. This request was granted, and within the next century provincial assemblies were introduced into most of the provinces of the East and West, primarily to conduct the services of the imperial cult and to celebrate games in honor of the deified emperor. But when the representatives of the several cities of a province met in their annual assembly, it was natural for them to discuss provincial affairs of general interest, and in particular to consider the conduct of the governor and the members of his staff. They never acquired the right to legislate for a province, but they exercised rather freely the right to call the attention of the governor and the emperor to conditions in the province, and in the late empire it seems to be clear from the *Theodosian Code* that they discussed questions of taxation, the public post, and cases of extortion by imperial officials. The members of these assemblies seem to have been true representatives of their respective cities, and not delegates with a mandate, and in one province, at least, Lycia, they were chosen by a system of proportionate representation. The Councils of the Church

were the natural successors of the provincial
assemblies. Like the assemblies they were
concerned primarily with religious matters.
The Provincial Council, meeting under the
direction of the Metropolitan, was made up
usually of the bishops of the province, but
not infrequently we find presbyters, deacons,
and laymen present, sent by their respective
cities, and from the close of the fifth century,
they, as well as the bishops, often vote. Marsiglio of Padua in the thirteenth century went
so far as to assert that a General Council
should be strictly representative of both
clergy and laity, and that a province should
have representatives according " to the number and quality " of its inhabitants, and in
the following century Occam worked out a
complete plan of representation for a Council.
It has been suggested by Dunning in his *History of Political Theories* that Marsiglio may
have based his proposal on the system which
he found in some of the medieval Italian cities. If that hypothesis is correct, we have a
double line of descent in the later period, at
least, for the representative idea. It matters
little that the political powers of the provincial assemblies were limited, or that the

bishops were the controlling element in the Councils of the Church; the essential facts are that representative government was well known to the Romans and that the representative principle survived in the assemblies and in the Church Councils until the Renaissance came to give it new life.

Probably no society has ever invented so many safeguards against Caesarism as the Roman oligarchy did. As we have already noticed, a candidate for a magistracy must have reached a specified age: he must hold the offices in a fixed order, and an interval of time must elapse before he can be re-elected to the highest office. His term was a short one, and during it his actions were always subject to the veto of his colleague. Another check upon him was furnished by the recall. This very new political device is as old as the tribunate of Tiberius Gracchus. It is an application of the doctrine of popular sovereignty in its extreme form, and grew out of earlier attempts to hold magistrates responsible for their conduct in office. The arguments which Gracchus used in support of his proposal to recall his colleague, Octavius, postulate the theory of popular sovereignty and sound sur-

prisingly like the considerations which are
urged by the supporters of the recall today.
According to Plutarch, Gracchus said: " We
esteem him to be legally chosen tribune who is
elected only by the majority of votes; and is
not therefore the same person much more law-
fully degraded, when by the general consent
of them all, they agree to depose him? " Perhaps we have not inherited the recall directly
from antiquity, but our acceptance of the
Roman doctrine of popular sovereignty has
led logically to the development of the recall,
as well as the initiative, and the referendum.

One of the characteristic features of a
Roman magistracy was the right which an incumbent had to veto the action of a colleague;
and the tribune had the right, which he freely
exercised, to veto the action of any other official. In some respects the Romans used the
veto power in a more practical way than we
do. Our governors, presidents, and other chief
executives may not interpose a veto until a
measure has been adopted and laid before
them for their signature. Often they are required to disapprove of long, important
measures, which they would gladly see adopted,
were it not for some slight defect. Under

Roman practice a bill could be vetoed before action had been taken upon it, or a tribune would ask for a night's delay before action should be taken. This arrangement gave proponents of a bill an opportunity to change the objectionable features of it. In recent years various timid excursions have been made into certain fields of political activity, in which Roman magistrates exercised their power freely. We try to influence the morals of people by exercising some supervision over the stage and over the public press; and in time of war the government has fixed the price of certain foods and attempted to provide for their proper distribution. What the censor's office did in its palmy days to improve the morals of the people and to check extravagance and display has been discussed in the last chapter, and in the aedile's office the Romans had a permanent Food Administration.

We have already observed that the political quality of the Romans which made for progress and stability at the same time more than did any other, was their ability to adapt old institutions to new conditions. In the practice of assigning a board of experts to an official we have an illustration of the way in which this result was accomplished. Probably no people in antiquity used experts so freely, and perhaps in modern times the practice is not so general as it was in Rome. A magistrate was elected directly by the people each year. He was better aware of the trend of popular sentiment than the average prime minister. He could confidently be expected to advocate progress or change. Attached to his office was a *consilium*, or body of expert advisers, who were familiar with precedent and usage and who would hold fast to the *mos maiorum*. In all departments of Roman public life such boards of advisers are to be found. The king, and later the consul, had the Senate as his *consilium*. The praetor, and, under the empire, the emperor had their *consilia* to assist them in the adjudication of cases, and in the field of the state religion the chief pontiff was advised by his board of pontiffs. The interaction of the forces which these two elements represented resulted in the gradual reform of old institutions, without too violent a break with law and tradition. We may regard the imperial bureaux which Hadrian brought to a state of perfection for the provinces as an extension of this system of government by experts.

The Roman theory of the relation of the state and the church runs through a cycle. The king was both chief executive and chief priest of the people. When the republic was established, priestly and political functions were dissociated, although all religious matters having a political significance were left to the magistrate. Julius Caesar in his dictatorship united in his person again the functions of the chief magistrate and chief pontiff, and this precedent was followed by all the emperors. The Emperor therefore held somewhat the same place in the state religion as the Czar did in Russia before the Revolution, and as the King does in England. This assumption of religious authority by the political ruler was the first step toward the recognition of the Divine Right of the Emperor; and the practice of paying divine honors to him, which, as we have noticed in Chapter I, was introduced from the Orient, fostered the development of the theory. In European countries the Roman practice of uniting the spiritual and temporal powers has survived in the form of a state religion or in the control of ecclesiastical affairs which most states have assumed in some measure. The United States, in enforcing a complete separation of State and Church, stands almost alone among the Great Powers in not accepting the Roman tradition.

One cannot bring to an end even a brief discussion of the influence which the executive and legislative branches of the Roman government have exerted on the political life of our own times without mentioning the remarkable revival which we have seen lately in Italian Fascismo, of the old Roman spirit and of certain Roman political institutions. In its purpose, its spirit, and its external form this movement revives pure Roman tradition. It began to attain its present great strength in the months immediately following the Armistice when there was a marked decline of national feeling and when disorder and class struggles were rife throughout Italy. It assumed the form of a great national movement when it broke the general strike of August 1, 1922, which threatened the orderly life of the whole nation. The Fascisti took this step after the government had failed to set the wheels of industry in motion again. The next step, the setting aside of parliamentary government and the assumption of the dictatorship by Signor Mussolini, the leader of the Fascisti, was inevitable. The whole course of events during the last six months of 1922 duplicates incidents common enough in early Roman history. Disorder arises throughout the peninsula or a great danger confronts the state. The ordinary methods of government are suspended, and a dictator is appointed to meet the emergency. The dictator in the olden time called the citizens to arms, just as Signor Mussolini assembled his one hundred and seventeen thousand armed followers at the Villa Borghese in the autumn of 1922. These men of today show the same spirit of unquestioning obedience to the state which characterized the Roman in olden time. One may well think himself back in the third century B. C., listening to the ancient Roman soldiers gathered before their dictator, when he reads the oath which the assembled Fascisti took in Rome on January 1, 1923: " I swear loyalty to Benito Mussolini, who governs the destinies of Italy. I swear devoted and absolute obedience to his government with uncontrolled conscience, which involves also the supreme sacrifice of life, the renunciation of all personal initiative,

[93]

and the daily practice of iron discipline."
That this movement was directly inspired by
Roman tradition is made plain by the symbols
and forms which it takes. It gets its name
from the *fasces*, or bundle of rods, which the
lictor carried, as a symbol of the authority
of the state, and the Fascista army is organized like the old Roman army into *manipuli,
centuriae, cohortes*, and *legiones*.[18]

Who can say what this reawakening of the
old Roman spirit may mean for Italy? It has
already given rise to a new *Risorgimento*. It
was the cause of Italy's participation in the
War and was the result of that War. Italy
bore her part of the burden of the War with
the other great Powers of Europe. She has
freed herself from the economic domination
of Germany and from the threat of Austrian
invasion. Her "Unredeemed Lands" are
restored to her. Her control of the Adriatic
seems assured. Out of these achievements
surged up the feeling of national independence
and solidarity embodied in the Fascista organization, which numbers now several hundred thousand young men, and at the same
time it was the Fasci or patriotic groups,
which came into existence in the early years

of the war, that made these achievements possible. The organization has set a bad precedent in its use of violent methods, and in establishing a military force outside the state. In its dealings with other peoples it may assert national ambitions too vigorously, but it bids fair to give expression to the national genius and to inspire Italy with a new life and vigor.

5. THE JUDICIARY

If one passes from the legislative and executive branches of the Roman government to the judicial, he thinks at once of Roman law, the greatest legacy which Rome has left us. With that subject we are not concerned in this book. But the judicial machinery of the Romans and some phases of their court procedure are of lively interest to one who is comparing Roman and modern institutions. Of most importance to us in this connection are the methods which the Romans followed in dealing with *crimina publica,* with what we may roughly, but somewhat inexactly, call criminal cases. For the hearing of such cases, by the early part of the first century before our era, the Romans had established eight or nine courts under the

presidency of praetors and ex-aediles.[19]   The
competence of these several courts was essentially different from that of our courts and
may well lead us to ask ourselves if our system
makes for efficiency.   One Roman court, for
instance, confined itself to hearing cases of
magistrates charged with extortion.   Others
heard respectively only cases of forgery, or of
treason, or of corrupt practices at elections,
or of peculation in office.   Under this system
each court was peculiarly qualified from long
experience to deal with the class of cases which
came before it.   Under our practice today
where cases of different sorts come before the
same judge, such special competence as the
Roman praetor and his board of trained jurists
attained can hardly be gained.   The praetor's
court continued to about the third century.
Under the later empire criminal cases were
heard in Italy by the city prefect or the
praetorian prefect, and in the provinces by the
governor.

The juries which sat with the praetor in
hearing criminal cases were much larger than
ours.   The smallest one of which we have any
record numbered thirty-two.   A case was
decided, as it is in most Continental countries

today, by a majority vote of the jurors. As used to be the practice in the Scottish courts, the Roman juror could vote that a charge was " not proven," but probably in the later period such ballots were counted for acquittal. The last extant reference to juries in Roman times is from the second century after Christ. This fact has led some modern writers to take it for granted that there is no connection between the Roman jury system and the modern one. Before medieval life had been studied carefully, this was a natural conclusion. Its character was not well understood, and Roman institutions were so modified in the Middle Ages that they were not easily recognized in their later forms. It is also true that, until very recent times, many who studied the origins of modern institutions did not raise their eyes above the modern horizon, or were led by national pride to find those origins among the peoples of their respective countries. This state of things is true, not only of the jury system, but in the case of other modern institutions, yet a more thorough and impartial historical investigation is giving to the Romans the credit which is due to them. We can do no more here than indicate very briefly the links which connect the modern jury system with the ancient one. The character of that system was indicated in the *Code* of Theodosius. Much of this *Code* was adopted in the *Breviary* of Alaric in 506 A.D. and in other summaries based in part on the Roman law, such as the *Capitularies* of the Merovingian and Carolingian kings. It is therefore a significant fact that under the Merovingians justice was administered by the Count, but on the verdict of the notables, called in the texts *rachimburgii* or *boni homines*. These *boni homines* were chosen by the Count, or judge, at the beginning of the hearing from the freemen assembled in the court. The minimum number chosen was seven. Feudalism put an end to the jury in France, and in its place cases were tried by ordeal, by battle, or by compurgation on the Continent. At this point two or three facts in the historical sequence are noteworthy. Our collection of the *Capitularies* was made in 827. Within a century the Normans made themselves masters of North Western France. They readily adopted French usages, and it is a fact admitted on all sides, since Palgrave's great work appeared a century ago, that the beginnings of the English jury system were brought into England by the Normans in the form of an inquest by sworn recognition. At first this method of deciding cases was accepted only as an alternative mode of trial. Twelve knights were selected who were required to declare on oath which contestant in their opinion had the better right. The Continental countries took over the jury from England after 1789. We are not concerned here with the many complex questions which arise in attempting to explain the development of the grand jury and the petty jury on English soil. The outstanding fact is that we owe the judge-and-jury system to the Romans.

One of the most extraordinary features of their judicial system was the fact that the Romans had no permanent public prosecutor. The bringing of criminal actions under the republic was left to private initiative, but there seem to have been enough ambitious politicians to prosecute cases, at least those cases which were likely to bring distinction to the successful prosecutor. Indeed on some occasions the praetor, before beginning a trial, was obliged to give a preliminary hearing to several lawyers who claimed the distinction of bringing the charge against the accused party. The merits and defects of such a system are obvious. Charges were likely to be pushed with vigor, because the reputation of an advocate depended on securing a conviction, and sometimes a patriotic citizen prosecuted a powerful politician when a public prosecutor would have hesitated to do so. But on the whole the plan did not work well. This was especially true when there was a political element in the case. In such circumstances the charge was usually brought by a political opponent, or what was worse still, a political supporter might put the defendant on trial and secure an acquittal, before a real prosecution could take place. Before being allowed to undertake the prosecution of Verres, the venal and tyrannical governor of Sicily, Cicero had to convince the presiding praetor that his claim to the right of conducting the case was better than that of Quintus Caecilius Niger, who had been quaestor of Verres, and hoped to secure the acquittal of his former superior. Such cases of collusion between the prosecutor and the defendant became so common, that a heavy penalty was imposed on those found guilty of it. Even under the empire, when the senate began to hear certain important cases, there was no permanent public prosecutor, but the senate designated members of its own body to conduct the prosecution and the defence. In these trials the senate functioned as a jury, and the presiding consul, as a judge. As the emperor gained a greater control of public affairs, it was not unnatural that he should take over criminal jurisdiction in important cases or delegate it to his prefects. When this point was reached, probably the prosecution of criminal actions was assumed more definitely by the state.

We frequently introduce " character witnesses " in our trials. The Romans went still further. A Roman defendant brought with him to the court as many prominent friends (*advocati*) as he could to make a favorable impression on the jury. In important cases today in America, although attorneys for the prosecution and defence sometimes give the jury brief outlines of the case before the evidence is presented, their formal pleas are not made until the evidence is in. Our method is inductive. Formal pleas were usually made in a Roman court before the testimony was given. Much can be said for the Roman plan.

Having the analyses of the case, as presented by the prosecution and defence, clearly in mind, the average juryman is perhaps better qualified to decide which theory is made more probable by the facts in the case and is in a better position to pick out the salient facts than he is when dealing with heterogeneous bits of evidence. The same looseness of procedure which characterized the meetings of the Roman Senate is found in the courts.[20] The jury was not under careful surveillance; demonstrations of approval and disapproval occurred, violent discussions were not always stopped, the rules of evidence were less strict than they are with us, and technicalities played a less important part. In some of these particulars Continental courts have inherited Roman practices more fully than Anglo-Saxon courts have. In consequence of their elimination of technicalities, the Romans brought important criminal cases to an end much more quickly than we do, and justice was cheaper than it is with us. In Anglo-Saxon courts hearsay evidence, the opinions of witnesses, and facts irrelevant to the issue are excluded by the presiding judge. These rules of evidence were not applied in Roman courts, and when the Continental countries reintroduced the jury system, they went back to the Roman practices in this matter, as we noticed a few years ago in the famous trial at Viterbo.

6. CONCEPTION OF CITIZENSHIP

i. IN TIMES OF PEACE

A jealous solicitude for the rights of the average citizen is a marked trait of the Roman character. A clear understanding of what the rights of the common man were and an ingrained purpose to protect him in the exercise of them determine the development of judicial procedure in Rome, of law, and of political organizations. Perhaps the Romans have bequeathed to us no greater heritage than their conception of citizenship. With them it was not a mere dogma of political philosophy, set forth in the writings of idealists or incorporated in general terms in declarations of rights. It was made a reality in everyday life by law, by tradition, and by political reforms. It finds expression in the first written law which the Romans had, that of the Twelve Tables, and five centuries later we hear an echo of it in the historic claim of St. Paul. This ideal has been before us through the ages, and has been an inspiration and a guide to every true leader of democracy. The laws of the Twelve Tables, of which mention has just been made, set down in written form and in great detail an orderly procedure, which must be followed in a judicial action, and thus informed a citizen of his rights, and laid an obligation on the state to see that they were observed. The Valerio-Horatian law a little later gave a citizen the privilege of appealing in a capital case to the popular assembly. The establishment of the tribunate provided a democratic official to safeguard him against the arbitrary action of a magistrate. The dictatorship, the " final decree of the senate," and the other devices which the state used under the republic to suspend the rights of citizens were either done away with or hemmed in by constitutional safeguards. Cicero brings his terrible indictment of the governor of Sicily to a fitting climax with the charge that Verres had caused a Roman citizen to be put to death, and turning to the man at the bar he cries: *si tu apud Persas aut in extrema India deprehensus, Verres, ad supplicium ducerere, quid clami-*

tares, nisi te civem esse Romanum?
It is true that there were many slaves in the
Roman world, and that many freemen within
its limits did not enjoy the full rights of
Roman citizenship until late in the imperial
period, but these facts do not weaken the
point in which we are interested here. Wher-
ever he went a citizen had behind him the
sovereignty of the Roman state. Any community which wronged him must make resti-
tution, or it would feel the heavy hand of
Rome. This Roman principle that a state may
protect its citizens even in a foreign land has
been accepted by modern nations and is
jealously observed by them. In fact international relations are concerned in large measure with the protection by a state of its
citizens or subjects residing in foreign countries.
Their passports certify to their citizenship.
They may appeal to their minister or ambas-
sador when they think themselves wronged,
and may look with confidence for the support
of the army and navy of their respective countries, when their lives, liberty, or property are
threatened.

ii. IN TIMES OF WAR

We have just been considering the fortunate position of the Roman citizen in times of peace. When wars arose, he became the servant of the state. Unlike the Carthaginians, the Romans did not during the periods of the Great Wars, employ mercenaries. Service in the army was compulsory on all citizens between seventeen and forty-six years of age who had property of a certain amount. Those who avoided service were liable to have their property confiscated, or to be sold as slaves, and desertion was a capital offence. Discipline was strict, and punishments were severe. But at the end of a campaign the soldier returned to civil life. Before the close of the third century B.C., however, the territory of Rome extended beyond the sea, and a soldier's term of service was correspondingly lengthened. This fact made the well-to-do, who were already disinclined to service in the army, still more opposed to it. This was the situation which led Marius to substitute voluntary enlistment for conscription toward the end of the second century. The new plan quickly filled the ranks of the army. The needy and the adventurous found a soldier's career attractive. They accepted it as their life's work. Their home was the camp. "*Esprit de corps* took the place of patriotism." As I have remarked in my *Roman Political Institutions:* " Henceforth the soldiers who came back to the city after protracted campaigns did not look on their commander, as their fathers had done, as a simple fellow-citizen, who had like themselves been serving the state, and now resumed his place by their side. Long periods of service abroad under the direction of one man had led them to follow implicitly the guidance of an individual." The veterans of Marius, of Sulla, of Pompey, and of Caesar could be trusted to follow at home the political leadership of the man under whom they had served abroad. This situation threw the control of politics into the hands of those who commanded the largest armies. What was still worse, the state could no longer count on the fidelity of its soldiers. Their allegiance had been transferred from Rome to their commander-in-chief, and the security of the government itself might depend on his loyalty or his lack of political ambition. From the begin-

ning of the first century before Christ to the
end of the empire the sinister figure of the
army is ever in the background. It was a
disturbing force in politics, as we have just
seen, by giving political offices and an undue
influence to military men without regard to
their fitness for political leadership, and by
organizing forcible interference with public
meetings of which the veterans disapproved;
and the claims which the soldiers made for
lands and bonuses often put the government in
a difficult position. Of some of these evils,
of which we have been painfully aware in this
country after our various wars, we shall have
occasion to speak in the next chapter. Fortunately in our history the army has never
threatened the existence of a stable government or been used to overthrow it, as it was
used in Rome in the year 68–69 and almost
constantly during the third century of our era.

7. TAXATION AND FINANCE

In the fields of taxation and public finance
we have not much to learn from the Romans,
save by way of warning. Most of the revenue
of the state came from the provinces, and for

several centuries was collected by tax-farmers.[21] We are familiar enough in more recent times with the exploitation of provinces, or colonies, as we call them, by the state or the great trading company, because most modern nations have followed Rome's policy of making their colonies subserve the interests of the mother country. In Sicily, the first overseas territory which the Romans acquired, they took over the system of taxation which they found in vogue there. That system rested on the Oriental theory that the land belonged to the sovereign, and that those who held the land paid rent for its use. This was the basis of taxation in all the later provinces also. Next in importance to the tribute were the customs duties. They brought in a large revenue, but were a great impediment to trade. Rome held almost all the civilized world. Consequently duties collected on the frontiers of the empire would not have amounted to much. What the Romans did was to divide the empire into tariff districts, and collect duties from those entering these districts. Trade suffered in consequence, as it did in France before the Revolution under similar conditions. The only other important tax in this connection was the five per cent inheritance tax imposed on property left to others than near relatives. It was instituted by Augustus, was levied on Roman citizens, and met with violent opposition. This system, taken in its entirety, relieved Italy from the burden of taxation.

The grant of Roman citizenship to practically all freemen in the provinces by Caracalla in 212 was therefore a severe blow to Italy, because it raised the provinces to the level of the peninsula, and paved the way for Diocletian to apply his fiscal reforms to the whole Roman world.[22] His system of taxation was one of the most complete and methodical that has ever been known. We can speak of only a few of its salient features here. The population was divided into three classes, the owners of land or other property, merchants, and laborers. For the first class, the class most important for the purpose of taxation, the fiscal unit was the *caput* or *iugum*. The *caput* was the working power of a man in good health. A *iugum* was a piece of land from which a fixed return might be expected. The number of *capita* and *iuga* was determined by a careful census at fixed intervals, and each land owner paid according to the number of laborers and *iuga* on his estate. The tax paid by merchants depended on the capital invested in their business. Laborers paid a poll tax. The plan was well thought out, but the failure of the government to reduce the valuation of property as the prosperity of the empire declined, and its inability to reduce its own expenses made the taxes an intolerable burden, and contributed largely to impoverish the people and ruin local self-government. The Roman system of taxation, with some modifications, continued in use after the dissolution of the Empire and exerts an influence on our modern systems. Duties were still collected on wares in transit at frontiers, at bridges and at other points on the public highways. A quota of the produce was required from the owners of land, and the property of those who died without leaving a will went to the crown. It is clear that most of the Roman taxes, for instance, customs duties, the inheritance tax, a tax on landed property, and a poll tax, have been taken over by us, and find a place in our modern systems of taxation.

The funds which came into the imperial treasury from the different sources mentioned above were spent mainly on the government of

the provinces, on roads, bridges, and other
public works, on religion, on the army and
navy, and on the city of Rome. It is impossible to find out the size of these different
items. It has been calculated that in the
early part of the first century the army cost
160,000,000 sesterces a year, a sum which,
with some hesitation, one may roughly estimate had the purchasing value of $8,000,000.
An imperial procurator in one of the provinces received an annual salary which ranged
from $3,000 to $15,000. The expense of
provincial government was tremendously increased from the second century on by the development of an elaborate bureaucratic system.
The outgo for the city of Rome included expenditures for the construction and mainte-
nance of public works, for religious purposes,
and to provide food and amusement for the
populace. We notice the absence from the
list of charges of certain items like appropria-
tions for education and charity which form an
important part of a modern budget.

Under the republic the control of finances
rested mainly with the senate; under the
empire it was divided between the emperor
and the senate. The republican system of

financial administration would seem to us very loose, and surprising in the case of so practical a people as the Romans. Under it the senate appropriated money for a period of five years to be used by the censors in the construction of public works, and lump sums were voted for expenditure by the other civil magistrates, and itemized accounts were not required of them. As happened in so many other matters, with the empire a better system of financial administration came in. The government collected most of the taxes through its own agents. The supervision of receipts and expenditures was more thorough, and we hear of something approaching an itemized budget. The lion's share of the revenues went into the imperial fiscus. The funds at the emperor's disposal were also materially augmented by the development of crown property and of the emperor's private fortune. Many large private estates were confiscated by the emperor, and many legacies were left to him. Indeed it was often a hazardous thing for a rich man to pass over the emperor in his will. The hereditary principle of succession was never formally recognized in the Roman constitution, but it was practically followed from

Augustus to Nero, so that the interesting distinction which we make today between crown property and the patrimony of the emperor was not adopted before the year 69.

The minting of Roman money had the same history as the control of the budget. The senate had charge of it under the republic. Under the empire the emperor directed the gold and silver coinage; the senate issued bronze coins. Two episodes in the history of Roman coinage are of interest to the student of modern economic conditions. If Professor Frank's conclusions in a recent number of *Classical Philology* [23] are correct, Rome had a real bimetallic standard from 340 to 150 B.C. This was maintained by changing from time to time the amount of metal entering respectively into the silver and bronze coins of the period in question. The Roman system did not, however, involve the free and unlimited coinage of both metals, because the state limited its issue of money to the estimated needs of the community. The other incident occurs under the empire. It has its parallel in the unlimited issue of paper money today by many European governments. The Roman government was hard pressed to meet its obligations. It did so by debasing the coinage. This process was carried so far that in the third century it refused to receive its own silver coins in payment of taxes. Constantine brought order out of this confusion, by making the gold *solidus* the standard. This coin became the parent of the gold coinages both of the East and the West. It was accepted by the barbarian states. From the time of Pepin it was struck in silver and was current until 1793. The modern French word *sou* is of course an abbreviation of its name.

8. IMPERIALISM

Of all Rome's achievements in the field of politics none was so far-reaching in its influence and so lasting in its effects as her conquest of the world and her successful government of it for five hundred years or more. With the story of her conquests we are not concerned here. But, as President Butler of Columbia University has said in his *Annual Report* for 1921: " No educated citizen of a modern free state can afford to ignore the lessons taught by the Roman Empire, which for centuries held together in a commonwealth that was both prosperous and contented peoples widely differing in religious faith, in racial origin, and in vernacular speech." How did she weld them all, Britons, Gauls, Spaniards, and Africans, into one people whose feeling of unity was so strong that even in the intervening centuries it has not died out altogether? No national heroes will ever supplant Trajan or Ovid in the hearts of the Roumanian people. When the Italians invaded Tripoli a few years ago they thought of themselves as following in the footsteps of their great ancestors, and a political cartoon which had wide vogue in Italy at the time of the war and did much to stimulate enthusiasm for it showed a shadowy Roman commander, perhaps Scipio, landing in Africa at the head of an Italian army. How few modern empires can hope to establish such traditions as these, so far as peoples of alien races and religions are concerned! That the Romans were more successful in developing a feeling of solidarity and loyalty throughout their empire than modern nations have been, we have the testimony from different points of view of such competent judges as Lord Cromer and Boissier. In his *Ancient and Modern Imperialism* Lord

[116]

Cromer says: "If we turn to the comparative results obtained by ancient and modern imperialists; if we ask ourselves whether the Romans, with their imperfect means of locomotion and communication, their relatively low standard of public morality, and their ignorance of many economic and political truths, which have now become axiomatic, succeeded as well as any modern people in assimilating the nations which the prowess of their arms had brought under their sway, the answer can not be doubtful. They succeeded far better." Elsewhere he remarks that "there has been no thorough fusion, no real assimilation between the British and their alien subjects, and, so far as we can now predict, the future will in this respect be but a repetition of the past."

Not only is this unparalleled achievement of the Romans worthy of notice from the historical point of view, but the methods of assimilation and government which gave them their success should be peculiarly interesting and instructive to us in these days of fierce national rivalry for the control of undeveloped lands and natural resources. It is only fair to say that the Romans were more successful among the semi-civilized peoples of the West than they were in the Greek East. It is also true that most of the peoples within the limits of the empire were of the white races, and that towards the dark races the Romans do not seem to have shown the same repugnance on the score of color which modern white peoples show. Furthermore, the acceptance of polytheism in the ancient world facilitated the amalgamation of two alien peoples, because each of them was tolerant of the religion of the other and readily received the other's deities into its pantheon, whereas, as we know, the monotheistic creeds of modern conquering peoples, like Christianity and Mohammedanism, stand as a barrier between the conquerors and the conquered. In addition to the concrete civilizing agencies which they employed, and which we shall have occasion to notice in a moment, we may find the grounds of their success in certain mental and political qualities and habits. The Romans were not idealists. Consequently they did not try to foist a new political and social system on a conquered people. Indeed they were intellectually phlegmatic and drew back from the task of thinking out a political system in its entirety. They lacked alertness of mind and were not much interested in political philosophy. Their policy at home and abroad was that of opportunism. When they acquired a new territory, therefore, they were content to introduce a few general arrangements and then allow the conquered people to go on living their own life, retaining their old religion, customs, practices, and local institutions. Besides adopting this wise policy of tolerance, in the best period of provincial government the Romans followed sound administrative principles. They established a graded civil service, with reasonable hope of promotion for competent officials. In this way they developed a corps of experienced administrators. They paid adequate salaries to provincial governors and their subordinates, and secured them reasonably well against removal on purely political grounds. The home government kept a close supervision of provincial officials, and courts were provided for the trial of charges brought against them. So far as we know, these wise principles for the government of dependencies were first put into application by the Romans, and few, if any, of our modern empires are observing them with the same care that certain Roman emperors did.[24]

Along with a good administrative system went protection of life and property and the gradual extension of Roman law. The patience and moderation of the Roman come out with special clearness in the last matter. In spite of the supreme regard in which he held his own law, the Roman allowed provincial cities of native origin to retain their own local codes. Only colonies were required to adopt Roman law, but, since the colony enjoyed special privileges, native communities were often eager to gain the status of colonies, and with that status went the willing acceptance of Roman law. The everyday life of the Spaniard or the African under Roman rule went on as it had before. He carried on his daily occupations as in the past. He worshipped his native gods, and took part in his city's traditional festivals and merrymakings. If some one infringed on his rights, he brought action under the old-time laws before magistrates of his own choosing. Some general changes, however, which came with Roman rule materially improved his condition. His taxes were usually less than they had been before the Romans came. His life and property were safer. Trade developed, and he saw his native town grow. This wise treatment tended in time to make the natives of the West look on the Roman government with a friendly eye.

But the Romans used positive agencies in civilizing and Romanizing newly conquered peoples. The most effective of these agencies were the building of roads, the introduction of Latin, and the founding of colonies. The success of modern imperialist states has been determined in large measure by their wise or unwise use of these means of developing a dependency and of binding it to the rest of the empire, but we have much to learn in all three of these matters from Roman methods. The first of the great Roman roads, the Appian Way, was built in 312 B.C., near the close of the conquest of Central Italy. It ran from Rome to Capua, and was soon extended to the port which today bears the name of Brindisi. Before the close of the second century B.C. four other great highways had been constructed connecting Rome with Genoa, Reggio, Rimini and other points in Northern Italy. From these trunk-lines, branch roads were then built to large towns not situated on the main highway. This network of roads connected all the important districts of Italy with one another and with Rome. Those who have seen the remains of the Appian Way or of other Roman roads know how well they were built. The policy which was adopted for Central Italy, for Southern Italy, and for Northern Italy, as section after section of the peninsula yielded to Roman arms, was carried into the provinces. A map of Spain, for instance, at the close of the reign of Augustus showing the system of roads laid out by his engineers proves how thorough the Romans were in their plans for the pacification of the country and the development of its resources. These roads in the provinces, like the Trans-Siberian railway, were built first of all for military purposes. They made it easy to send troops and supplies to all parts of the empire. But they served a larger purpose in facilitating trade, in bringing remote regions into closer communication with one another and with Rome, and in developing a common way of living and of thinking throughout the world. In other words they helped to make the empire a unit. Even after the political bonds which held the Empire together had been relaxed, the roads were left. They made trade and travel possible. They furnished a ready means of communication between different parts of the world, and exerted a powerful influence in preserving for us the features of Roman civilization.[25]

One reason why the Romans surpassed modern imperialist states in their use of this effective civilizing agency is the fact that they employed their legionaries and auxiliaries in times of peace in the construction of roads and other public works. The story of the Third Augustan Legion in Africa, as Reid outlines it in his *Roman Municipalities,* is illuminating.[26] This legion was stationed in Northern Africa for a century and a half or two centuries, and from the numerous inscriptions which the French have brought to light there we can see the beneficent results of its labors throughout the province. In addition to the roads which it built, and the chains of forts, which it constructed along the frontier, there were at least five large towns which owed their construction almost entirely to the soldiers of the Third Legion. They developed the town of Theveste and constructed all the public buildings in it. When the surrounding country became peaceful and prosperous, the legion moved on to a new outpost, always enlarging the sphere of Roman influence. This is the history of Timgad. At first it was a military post, established to check raids by nomad tribes through the mountains. The soldiers constructed temples, baths, and all the other public buildings needed in a Roman city, and by 100 A.D. its importance was recognized by its elevation to the proud position of a Roman colony. In all parts of the Empire we find inscriptions recording the building by the soldiers of roads, bridges, amphitheatres, aqueducts, and harbors. Whether soldiers in modern times could be used for such purposes is doubtful, but we can at least see in the use which the Romans made of their soldiers one reason for their success as empire-builders.

In another way the soldiers played an important part in Romanizing newly conquered territory. Near every important garrison *canabae*, or settlements of merchants and camp-followers, sprang up. Many of the auxiliaries married native women, who made their homes in these villages. At the end of their term of service these foreign soldiers were made Roman citizens. Their marriages with native women were legalized, and they settled down in these communities on the frontier, to introduce Roman ideas and Roman institutions in the surrounding country. When we remember that there were probably 200,000 auxiliary troops in the second century, we can readily understand what a great influence their settlement in the provinces must have had. In this connection it is convenient to speak of the " organizations of Roman citizens," or the *conventus civium Romanorum,* as they were called. As soon as a new province had been acquired, Roman bankers, merchants, ship-owners, and publicans went to it and settled in the important cities. They quickly formed an organization of their own in the community where they lived, because it was natural for Romans to form a political or social organization, and because certain rights and privileges which they had set them off from the rest of the community. They made up the aristocracy of the towns where they lived, and many natives must have been spurred on to accept Roman ideas and attain Roman citizenship for the sake of being enrolled in the *conventus.* The trade which these merchants carried on, and which a fine system of roads made possible, had a levelling influence throughout the Empire. Italy and Gaul sent their pottery and bronze utensils, Syria its silk and linen, Egypt its cotton goods and ivory, and Arabia its gums and spices to all the great centres of the world. The articles of everyday use and many articles of luxury were, therefore, the same in all the provinces, and must have had a great influence in making the daily life of all the people under Roman rule uniform. Trade usually " followed the flag," but in some cases enterprising Roman merchants went in advance of it. Trajan found them in the capital of Parthia when he took that city, and there was an " organization of Roman citizens " in Alexandria long before Rome established a protectorate over Egypt.

In his *Ancient and Modern Imperialism* Lord Cromer remarks: " Modern Imperialist nations have sought to use the spread of their language in order to draw political sympathy to themselves. This has been notably the case as regards the French in the basin of the Mediterranean, and — though perhaps less designedly — as regards the English in India. I do not think that either nation is likely to attain any great measure of success in this direction. They will certainly be much less successful than the Romans. Neither in French, British, nor, I think I may add, Russian possessions is there the least probability that the foreign will eventually supplant the vernacular languages." Elsewhere he says: " (My) conclusion is that the great proficiency in some European language often acquired by individuals amongst the subject races of the modern Imperialist Powers in no way tends to inspire political sympathy with the people to whom that language is their mother tongue. . . . Indeed, in some ways, it (i.e., language) rather tends to disruption, inasmuch as it furnishes the subject races with a very powerful arm against their alien rulers." This frank confession by a competent authority that the languages of the dominant nations are not making much progress among the subject races, and that proficiency in them tends often to alienate the conquered people from their rulers, a fact which we have seen illustrated lately in the case of the leaders of the revolutionary movements in India, brings into striking relief not only the remarkable success which the Romans had in making Latin the

common language of the western world but also
the effective use which they made of it in unifying the Empire. In two chapters of my book on
The Common People of Ancient Rome I have
tried to show what the nature of this language
was and how it spread through the Empire.[27]
In Dacia, or modern Roumania, for instance,
a province beyond the Danube, which the
Romans held for only one hundred and
seventy-five years, Latin was so firmly
established that it has persisted in its modern
form to the present day. In his *Romanization of Roman Britain* Haverfield has shown
for this remote province from a study of the
ephemeral inscriptions on bricks and tiles
that " Latin was employed freely in the
towns of Britain, not only on serious occasions or by the upper classes, but by servants
and work-people for the most accidental
purposes." The missionaries who carried
it throughout the ancient world were the
soldier, the colonist, the trader, and the
official. It surprises one to find out, also, that
all classes could not only speak Latin, but
could read and write it. Across the Empire
from Britain to Dacia it is the same story.
On the tombstones of the petty merchant and

the freedman, as well as on the bronze tablets which contain laws and decrees, the language is Latin, and essentially the same Latin as one would hear in the city of Rome. It is clear that modern Imperialist states have much to learn from the methods which Rome employed so successfully in furthering the use of her language by subject races. Lord Cromer regrets the fact that acquaintance with the tongue of the ruling people often becomes in modern times a weapon which is turned against that people. In the Roman provinces it conferred distinction, opened the way to fuller rights and privileges and made the possessor of it a stronger supporter of the Roman régime.

Nothing brings out better the great contrast between the individualism of modern times and the solidarity of the Roman commonwealth than a comparison of the methods followed now and two thousand years ago in settling an undeveloped country.[28] Reports of the great resources of Alaska come to Oregon and Colorado and New York. Men from all quarters hurry there indiscriminately. On some promising location a village grows up, almost over night. It has no magistrates, no common council. Some of the more public-spirited citizens gradually band themselves together to preserve order and dispense a rude justice. In time a municipal government is organized. The Roman method of occupying a new territory was far different from this. It consisted primarily in the establishment of colonies in the new region. The most desirable locations for strategic and commercial reasons were picked out, and a law was passed in the popular assembly authorizing the establishment of a colony, and providing for commissioners to found it. From three hundred to several thousand colonists were then enrolled, and marched out in military order to the chosen site. The commissioners assigned the allotments, drew up a charter for the new community, and appointed its first magistrates and the members of the local senate. This compact and highly organized community of Romans served as a military outpost and a centre for the extension of Roman civilization. The complete pacification and Romanization of Italy was largely due to the influence of these colonies. More than four hundred and forty such communities were established in Italy and the provinces. Modern empires have much to learn from this feature of Roman policy, and it would almost seem as if we were beginning to appreciate its value. The State of California has in late years adopted a system of colonization closely resembling the Roman. It selects a site, appoints experts to subdivide the land, chooses the colonists carefully, and sends the colony out under a board of directors. Under a measure proposed by the United States Secretary of the Interior, Secretary Lane, a year or two ago, but not yet adopted by the Congress, similar settlements were to be established on government land by the coöperation of the federal and state governments. An interesting experiment along Roman lines, but under private auspices, was made in July, 1921, when an organized band of selected colonists set out from Brooklyn to found a settlement in Idaho, with the coöperation of that state.[29] The advantages which the Roman plan has over our ordinary method of settling a new region are apparent at once.

A discussion of this feature of the policy which the Romans followed in a newly acquired territory naturally leads us to speak of their attitude toward native communities. Lord Cromer remarks that the Roman provinces did not have self-government. It is true that Spain and Gaul did not have their own legislatures and chief magistrates, but the real administrative units with which Rome dealt in making her arrangements were the city-states of Spain and Gaul, and they had a large measure of self-government conferred on them by their charters. In a province like Spain one finds communities in all the different stages of advancement from the position of a dependent village to a free city or a Roman colony, and one may well ask if the Roman system was not a more practical one than ours. We treat Porto Rico, for instance, as a unit. All the villages or cities in the island are put on the same legal basis, no matter what the state of civilization of the different towns may be. The Romans would have granted the full rights of citizenship to one or two of them, and advanced the others from their more lowly state as they became more civilized and prosperous. In this way they held before native communities a prize which those communities were always eager to attain, and from the first century of our era we find one town after another advancing to a fuller enjoyment of civic rights. The same policy was applied to individuals. Roman citizenship was often granted to selected persons in a community. Such a grant identified the interests of these provincial leaders with those of Rome, and enlisted their support for the Roman régime.

The agencies which the Empire used so successfully in Romanizing the provinces, that is to say the establishment of law and order, the retention of local self-government, the liberal grants of citizenship to qualified individuals and cities, the development of a good civil service, the building of roads, the construction of public works, the introduction of the Latin language and of Roman law, and the unifying influence in the later period of the Church, engendered a feeling of solidarity throughout the Western World, which was one of the most valuable legacies handed down by the Romans to later times. Even Claudian, the last important Roman poet, writing after the crushing defeat of Valens by the barbarians at Adrianople, saw clearly that, in spite of all the disasters which had overtaken Rome, the sense of unity still persisted throughout the Western World. He writes in sorrow of the goddess, Roma:

" Her voice is weak, and slow her steps; her
eyes
Deep sunk within; her cheeks are gone;
her arms
Are shrivelled up with wasting leanness,"

but at another moment he cries triumphantly:
" We who drink of the Rhone and the Orontes
are all one nation." The feeling which
Claudian expresses persisted throughout the
Middle Ages. The German states in Italy
recognized it by putting the portrait of the
Eastern Emperor on their coins. As Poole
remarks in his *Illustrations of the History of
Mediaeval Thought:* " The Empire of Charlemagne was no mere resuscitation of the extinct empire of the West. It was the continuation of that universal empire, whose seat
Constantine had established at Byzantium,
but whose existence there was now held to
have terminated by the succession of a woman,
the empress Irene. . . . The empire, therefore,
went back to its rightful seat, and its title
devolved on Charlemagne." All the minor
rulers also throughout the civilized parts of
Europe thought of their authority as coming to
them from the Roman Empire. This feeling

of unity was kept up by the use of the old Roman highways of commerce, by the employment of the Latin language as the *lingua franca* of Europe, by the Church, and by the continued use of Roman law. Roman law in particular was a stabilizing influence for many centuries after the dissolution of the Empire. In the East and in the portions of Italy controlled by Justinian's successors the *Code* of Justinian was in force. Roman law entered largely also into the *Breviary* of Alaric, the laws of the Burgundians, the edict of Theodoric, and the French capitularies. The law of Justinian was taught in the schools of Rome and Ravenna without much interruption from the sixth to the eleventh century, and with the revival of commerce which followed the Crusades, there was a vigorous development of Roman mercantile law. After the tenth century " the trend was toward unity within certain areas and the political separation of these great areas from each other." This drift toward nationalism reached its climax at the time of the Reformation. The spirit of a larger unity, which earlier centuries had taken over from the Roman Empire, disappeared in great measure, but the longing for it and the need of it and the knowledge that it once existed and may be called to life again, find expression today in the organization of the League of Nations. How disastrous has been its displacement by the present intense nationalistic spirit is recognized on all sides. It would almost seem as if Philip Kerr, who had served as Confidential Secretary of Lloyd George at the Peace Conference in Paris, was thinking of the irreparable loss which Europe has suffered in this respect, when he said in his address at the Williamstown Conference in 1922: "What is the fundamental cause of war? I do not say the only cause of war, but the most active and constant cause. It is not race or religion or color or nationality or despotism, or progress, or any of the causes usually cited. It is the division of humanity into separate states. The proposition which I am concerned to establish today is the division of humanity into separate states, each owing loyalty to itself, each recognizing no law higher than its own will, each looking at every problem from its own point of view, which is the fundamental cause of war." Rome welded the particularism of the ancient

Mediterranean world into the unity of her Empire. Only by a similar recognition of the solidarity of the interests of all civilized peoples can we hope to emerge from the conditions which threaten us today.

III. SOME POLITICAL AND SOCIAL PROBLEMS COMMON TO THE ROMANS AND TO MODERN PEOPLES

THE political and social problems which confronted Rome are those which America, England, and France face today, and nothing brings out more clearly the close relation which our civilization bears to hers than the identity of these ancient and modern problems. In no respect may we profit more by a study of her history than in contemplating the means which Rome employed in solving them. Her successes may guide us, and her failures warn us. Some of the difficulties which beset her have come to the surface in discussing certain topics in the two preceding chapters, and of the others we can speak briefly of only a few, and mainly by way of illustration.

1. THE COLOR AND THE LABOR QUESTIONS

Two of our most serious social and political questions do not come to the surface in Roman history, at least not in the form in which they present themselves today. I mean the " color question " and the labor question. Lord Cromer in the book to which reference has already been made ventures the opinion that " antipathy based on differences of colour is a plant of comparatively recent growth." He connects its development with the fact that in modern times the white man has enslaved only the black man. Out of this relation the hostility of the two races has developed, and has extended its scope so as to determine in some measure the attitude of the white man toward the brown and yellow man. The Roman had both white and black slaves. All foreigners were on the same plane below himself. Consequently he did not have that difficulty in dealing with the dark races which some modern nations experience.

In the towns and villages of the Roman Empire we find inscriptions attesting the existence of nearly five hundred different trade-guilds.[30]   Industry was carried to a high degree of specialization. We find organizations of carpenters, joiners, gold-smiths, silver-smiths, sandal-makers, bakers, skippers, actors, gladiators, and of men in almost every conceivable occupation. Yet we have no record of an industrial strike in Roman history,[30a] nor of the intrusion of the labor question into politics. The Roman trade-guilds do not seem to have tried to raise wages or to improve working conditions, in spite of their great numbers and their large membership. They were primarily benevolent and social societies. Most of the laborers worked in their own homes or in small shops, and not in large factories where common conditions develop class consciousness and a sense of solidarity. Furthermore, the great majority of the manual laborers were either slaves or freedmen, and joint action to improve their condition would have been well nigh impossible.

2. Voting and Elections

Passing now to a discussion of some of the political and social problems which the Romans and modern peoples *do* have in common, we may conveniently begin a comparative study of these questions by saying a word about the way in which the Romans tried to suppress the evils connected with canvassing for votes and conducting the elections. The simplicity and strictness of the olden time is well illustrated by the earliest corrupt-practices acts, which forbade candidates for public office to whiten their togas or to go about among the farmers on market days. Next we hear of an edict to prevent two candidates from combining against a rival. Not until the second century B.C., when wealth from the provinces began to pour into Rome, do we find laws against bribery on the statute books. From this time on proof multiplies that fraud and force were used at the elections. Between 67 and 52 B.C. no less than six bills were brought in to suppress political corruption. The two evils which were most prevalent were the formation of corrupt political clubs and the excessive expenditure of money by candidates. Aspirants for office spent enormous sums in giving gladiatorial games and public banquets. We hear a great deal about political clubs in the *Candidate's Handbook* which Quintus Cicero addressed to his brother in 64 B.C., when Marcus was a candidate for the consulship. These organizations were formed by ambitious politicians for the purpose of controlling the elections by bribery or the use of force. They broke up the political meetings held by candidates of the opposite party, blocked up the entrances to the polling booths, gave out only ballots of their own party, and openly canvassed for voters who could be bribed. The Romans had even less success in combatting these evils by means of legislation than we have had. Not until the elections had been transferred from the people to the senate did they disappear. The remedies which helped most in holding them in check were the introduction of the secret ballot, the establishment of a special court to hear cases of bribery, with the power to inflict severe penalties, and the suppression of all political clubs. This last measure was very helpful, but it was easier of adoption in Rome, where the right of association was limited, than it would be today. Cicero's contemporary, Cato, made the interesting proposal that all newly chosen magistrates should be required to appear in court and prove that they had been elected by legitimate means, but this bill failed of passage.

Money was freely used by unscrupulous aspirants for office, but it is not probable that capital played the important part in directing the policy of the state which certain modern writers ascribe to it. The suppression of piracy in the Eastern Mediterranean and the restoration of order in Asia Minor by Pompey were undoubtedly brought about by the influence of the bankers and tax-farmers, but two or three important considerations make it reasonably certain that " big business " did not have the political power in Rome which it has with us today.[31] The amount of money invested in public contracts was comparatively small. Even under the Republic only a small part of the revenue from the provinces was collected by private Roman companies, and under the Empire, as we have already noticed, the collection of taxes was taken over more and more by the state. Finally, there do not seem to have been many large financial corporations, and there is little, if any, evidence to show that they combined to bring pressure to bear on the government. In fact, Roman business and trade were largely individualistic.

3. THE POLITICAL BOSS

In the last century B.C. political and social conditions were ideal for the development of the political boss, and in many respects they resemble our own. In the first place, Rome, as is the case with many of our large cities today, was filled with foreigners. We shall have occasion later to discuss in greater detail the social and economic effect of the presence in Italy and Rome of this foreign population. For our present purpose it is sufficient to note that Professor Frank in a recent number of the *American Historical Review* [32] has shown that nearly 90 per cent. of the population permanently resident at Rome in the Empire were of foreign extraction. Most of these foreigners were of course slaves, but many were freedmen who had the right to vote. They were ignorant of Roman political traditions. Many of them made a precarious living, and their votes could probably be had for money or through the influence of their patrons. Of such men the guilds and political clubs of the late Republic were largely made up. To them we must add the freemen who were driven out of the country districts by the decline of agriculture, or who drifted to the city because of the attractions which it could offer. These classes of people naturally fell under the leadership of political bosses. It happened too that several of the political bosses of this period had been or were still in command of large armies. Veterans who had served under these commanders and had settled in Italy naturally accepted the political leadership of their former officers. We are familiar in this country with the great influence exerted at the end of several of our wars by compact organizations of ex-service men. Furthermore, in Rome there were no permanent party organizations. Voters followed a leader, rather than a political principle. All these facts contributed to strengthen the hands of the boss, and the political history of the last half century of the Republic centres about the activity of such men as Marius, Crassus, Caesar, Milo, and Clodius. Indeed the First Triumvirate, which controlled Rome for ten years, had no legal basis. It rested upon a personal agreement between Caesar, Pompey, and Crassus for the division of the political spoils. In a certain degree Augustus con-

[145]

tinued this tradition, for his power rested largely upon the fact that the candidates for office favored by him were certain to be elected and would do his bidding after the election, and thus the measures supported by him were sure to be adopted. The Roman boss differed from most political bosses of today in his willingness to take office and assume the responsibility which the holding of an office entails.

The political boss is of course abhorrent to an oligarchical system. It is a fundamental principle of an aristocracy that no individual should attain undue prominence above others of his class, and perhaps no governing body has devised so many safeguards against Caesarism, and entrenched itself so firmly behind tradition, as the Roman senate did. Every aspirant for an important magistracy must have reached a specified age and must have held all the lower offices. These provisions prevented a successful politician from being carried into the consulship on a sudden wave of popular favor, and a consul's term of office was so short that he had little opportunity to make his political position secure. Over against him stood the senate with its *esprit de corps,* and its power to control appointments and to ratify or reject treaties, which, as we noticed in the last chapter, enabled it to determine in large measure his domestic and foreign policy. The Roman Senate protected itself for many decades against the political aspirations of successful generals by granting them or withholding from them a sufficient army, by voting them generous or niggardly apropriations, by requiring them to submit all their acts to it for ratification, and by conceding to them or refusing them a triumph or a " thanksgiving " on their return to Rome. Its power was only broken in the last century of the Republic when certain democratic magistrates made an appeal directly to the popular assembly. To this move on the part of the Executive we have had an analogue on several occasions when the Chief Executive of the United States or of a state has made a popular appeal to the voters in his struggle with a legislative body.[33]

4. THE RECALL

One of the political problems with which we have been much concerned in late years has to do with the possibility of removing an elected official from office. We proceed to the accomplishment of that purpose in two ways, by the traditional method of impeachment or by the new device of the recall. They differ in the fact that the former is a judicial procedure, whereas a recall is brought about by the direct action of the voters. The Romans were a practical people and did not like to interfere with the orderly transaction of public business by removing an executive from office. Consequently we have no record of any attempt being made to remove a civil magistrate from office until we come to the stormy period of the second century before our era. In 169 B.C. one of the censors of that year was impeached and tried before the popular assembly, and in 133 B.C. the tribune Tiberius Gracchus secured the recall of his colleague Octavius by a popular vote. Both cases illustrate the application of the Roman doctrine of popular sovereignty in its extreme form. Neither method of procedure, however, found favor in later years. In fact the Romans did not have so much need of either process as we have today, because the tribune could veto an arbitrary or unscrupulous act of a magistrate.

5. PENSIONS, BONUSES, AND MILITARISM

One of the important political and economic questions which countries have to settle in modern times at the close of a war is that of reinstating soldiers in civil pursuits and of granting them some material compensation for their services. After the Civil War in this country the question was solved by throwing open lands in the Middle West to settlement and by appropriating money liberally for pensions. At the moment of writing the needs of the soldier returning to civil life from the late war with the Central European powers have been met in part by a system of insurance, by the payment of a small sum on discharge, and by making provision for the disabled. It has been further proposed to compensate men honorably discharged from service by giving them either cash payments or homestead allotments. All of these plans were tried by the Romans. Down to the close of the second century before our era only the well-to-do were enrolled in the legions. Marius for the first time opened the ranks to the proletariat. When the term of service of his soldiers came to an end he had to make suitable provision for them. He did so by founding a colony and granting them allotments in it. This precedent was followed by Sulla, Pompey, and Caesar, and between 59 and 31 B.C. twenty-five or thirty colonies of veterans were thus established. Under the Empire a soldier received also a fixed sum of money on his discharge. The benefit societies which the Roman government encouraged among the soldiers served somewhat the same purpose as our system of war-insurance. The bonus system was adopted, in a formal way, for the first time by Augustus in 7 B.C., instead of the customary assignments of land. At that time he gave gratuities to his discharged soldiers amounting to 400,000,000 sesterces, as he tells us in his biography.[34] Although this is perhaps the earliest instance of the systematic award of a large cash payment, occasional grants of this sort occurred much earlier, because the bonus had its beginning in the division of the spoils of war among the soldiers, and was given at the time of the triumph. When the practice of granting a bonus had once been formally established, the occasions on which it was given were multiplied for political reasons. To win popularity with the army, Tiberius, on his accession, made a grant of money to every soldier, and his example was followed by Caligula, Claudius, Nero, and most of their successors. In the later empire, when the support of the army became all-important to an emperor, bonuses increased in size; they were given on many anniversaries, and imposed a very heavy burden on the imperial treasury. In the fourth century the Emperor Julian, who was far from warlike, on mounting the throne, gave to every Roman soldier a bonus whose nominal value was equal to about thirty-two dollars. Since there were probably 400,000 soldiers in the army, this action cost the government $12,800,000 or nearly $50,000,000 if we roughly estimate that gold and silver would purchase four times as much then as they do now. The militaristic spirit of Rome has descended to us and makes its influence felt today. The campaigns and the conquests of great Roman commanders have been studied with minute care by generals and statesmen in modern times. Elaborate studies, for instance, have been made of Caesar's campaigns by Napoleon III, by Col. Stoffel of his staff, and

[151]

in General von Göler's great work dedicated
to Marshall von Moltke with the noteworthy
phrase: "Feldherr und Sieger auf gallischem
Boden." Elsewhere, in a paper on the trend
of classical history, I noted the fact that the
study of Roman military history had been
engaging the attention of an unusually large
number of scholars in the years immediately
preceding the war with the states of Central
Europe. It was also a significant thing that
many of these writers in their appraisal of
the men and the events of ancient times
tacitly held to the principle that in the ultimate analysis the course of history was determined by the use of naked force, and that the
progress of the world was furthered by the
conquest of the small nation by the great one.

6. Cases of Paternalism

In one of the preceding chapters we have
tried to show how the Romans in the second
century before our era attempted to check
the decline of morals and the growth of extravagance by giving the censor extraordinary
discretionary power over the daily life of the
citizens. It may be interesting in this connec-

tion to say a word of three or four other cases
of paternalism, in which the state interfered
in private life or business in the hope of correcting some widespread evil or social disorder.
All of these social evils which Rome tried
to remedy have their analogues in our own
times. The most outstanding of these problems was unemployment and lack of food in the
large cities. This was the problem which Gaius
Gracchus tried to solve by his corn law in
123 B.C. Our best estimates put the population of Rome at 800,000 in the early Empire.[35]
Perhaps it numbered a half million in the time
of the Gracchi. Italy, after supplying her own
needs, was unable to provide all these people
with sufficient food, or with food at prices
within the reach of the poor. In times of
great scarcity previous governments had tried
to meet the difficulty by bringing grain to
Rome from Sicily and Sardinia. The motives
which actuated them were not primarily
humanitarian. But a hungry proletariat would
have threatened the existence of society and
government. Gaius Gracchus tried to do in a
systematic way what some of his predecessors
had attempted in an irregular fashion. He
organized the purchase and transportation of

grain from the provinces and provided for its
sale at about half the market price. He may
have thought of this measure as a temporary
palliative to meet an emergency. He may have
hoped later to do away with unemployment,
by developing the industries of Rome and
settling the needy in colonies. He may have
expected to stimulate agriculture in Italy and
in that way to bring down the price of food.
But the immediate result was the recognition
by the state of its duty to provide food for the
city, and to adjust the price of the necessities
of life to the purse of the consumer. Within
seventy-five years after the tribunate of
Gracchus we hear of four or five new corn laws,
each one increasing the amount of grain supplied by the government or lowering its price.
The democratic leader, Clodius, in 58 B.C.
even supplied grain free to the needy.
Suetonius tells us that Caesar introduced a
partial reform by cutting down the number of
people who received cheap or free grain from
320,000 to 150,000. This essay in the fixing
of prices by the government which Gracchus
made in 123 B.C. was carried to its logical conclusion by Diocletian in his famous edict in
301 A.D. In another place the present writer

has made a study of this decree, which was found in Asia Minor some two centuries ago engraved on tablets.[36]   It is sufficient to note here that in this document the Emperor fixed the maximum prices which it was lawful to charge for seven hundred or eight hundred different articles comprising food, clothing, shoes, and labor of all kinds.   The penalty for selling an article at a higher price than that specified in the law was death.   The attempt to enforce the law led to riot and disorder and its ultimate repeal.

It will be noticed that in his edict Diocletian tried to fix wages, not minimum, but maximum wages.   The later empire was much concerned with the labor-question.   It believed that the prosperity of the people required a proper diversification of industry, that each community should have a sufficient number of carpenters, weavers, and farmers, for instance.   This end could be attained most easily by making an occupation hereditary in a family.   When this point had been reached the caste system was fixed on Roman society.   This final result may be seen in the *Theodosian Code* of the fifth century, but we cannot follow all the steps by which it was reached.   Apparently the state accomplished its purpose by means of the trade-guilds. Hundreds of inscriptions testify to the existence of these organizations in various parts of the Empire. Just as the central government made the *curia*, or local senate, responsible for the taxes of the municipality which it represented, so it held the guilds of carpenters or of weavers responsible for the services which they were qualified to render to the community. This obligation was first laid on the guilds of the skippers and bakers. If they allowed their trades to languish, Rome, Alexandria, and Constantinople would starve. Their occupations were the " basic industries " of antiquity. The man who was a baker or a seaman was therefore obliged to continue as a baker or seaman his life long, and his children were obliged to follow his footsteps. Gradually other trades were swept into the government's net, until freedom in industry and commerce had disappeared.

Even before the state had brought the laborer under its control, it had acquired the ownership of a great part of the natural resources of the Empire. The Emperor owned gold mines in Dalmatia and Dacia, silver mines in Pannonia, iron mines in Noricum, tin mines in Britain, and marble quarries, forests, clay-pits, and salt-works in other provinces. Egypt was from the outset the personal domain of the Emperor, and by confiscation or legacy he gradually acquired immense estates in most of the richer provinces. Most of the mines and the imperial estates were in charge of a procurator, and were let out at a fixed rental to contractors. The work on the estates was done by tenants. Whether state ownership promoted productivity or not we can not say with certainty, but the complaints which we find in the *Theodosian Code* [37] of the exorbitant prices charged for the products of the mines and quarries would seem to show that they were inefficiently managed under the later empire. The outcome, so far as the workers in the mines and the tenants on the estates are concerned, is clear enough. Titles are found in the *Theodosian Code*, [38] requiring those who live near the mines and their children to work in the mines. The condition of the tenants on imperial estates had fallen to a low point as early as the latter part of the second century, as we can see from the pathetic petition which the people on an imperial estate in Africa addressed to Commodus.

In time the tenants on these estates found it impossible to give up their leases, or were forbidden to do so, and became serfs.

In this field of paternalism of which we have been speaking another important issue of modern times has its counterpart in the history of Roman politics. I mean the attitude of the central government toward the municipalities within its territory. Within recent years this question has taken an acute form in the states of New York, Pennsylvania, and Illinois. To what extent may the legislature or the governor interfere to correct local evils in the city of New York, in Pittsburgh, or in Chicago? The Romans under the Republic were not much concerned with the welfare of the cities under their control. With the establishment of the Empire a change in their attitude is noticeable. The improvement in the general administration of the provinces naturally brought into relief certain evils in the local governments of provincial cities, especially financial mismanagement. The letters which Pliny, the governor of Bithynia, wrote to Trajan in the early part of the second century are very illuminating in this respect. He asks his imperial master what shall be done at Nicaea, where 10,000,000 sesterces have been spent on an unfinished theatre whose walls have already begun to crack.[39] May he inspect the accounts of the city of Apamea? Is it proper for him to check the extravagance shown at civic festivals? Out of these comparatively small beginnings there developed the imperial policy of supervising the finances of the municipalities of the Empire, and curators were sent out to them, who took entire charge of all the land and other property belonging to a city, and were responsible not to the citizens of the town, but to the governor of the province. The exercise by the curator of these large powers encroached on the authority of the local officials, lessened the feeling of civic responsibility among the people, and in the end completely undermined local self-government. If we make a possible exception of the censorship of morals in the second century before our era, all the experiments in paternalism which the Romans made failed:— the fixing of prices, the control of the labor market, state ownership, and the supervision of local government.

7. GROWTH OF CITIES

The drifting of large numbers of people into
the great cities was one of the baffling problems
of antiquity, as it is today. It meant the
withdrawal of farmers and farm-laborers
needed on the land. It led to unemployment
in the cities. It brought so many people into
the cities that it was difficult to supply them
with sufficient food. It made the cities in times
of economic distress or political excitement
dangerous centres of disorder. To discuss
here all the reasons why Rome and certain
other cities grew to their unwieldy size would
take us too far afield. We may mention, however, one or two of the influences at work.
Many of the native farm laborers had been
killed in the long wars. Many of the farmers
had suffered the same fate, and their farms
had passed into the hands of large landowners
and were cultivated by slaves. The remaining
peasant proprietors could not compete with the
ranch owners, and the free laborers could not
hold their own against the slaves. People
from both these classes went into the provinces or moved to the city in the early period,

while under the late republic and the empire
the size of the city was augmented by a great
influx of slaves, who found it a comparatively
easy matter to purchase their freedom or to
obtain it in the wills of their masters. To feed
these people and keep them reasonably contented the government gave them food free
or at a low price and provided them with baths,
theatres, and gladiatorial contests.   This
attempt to relieve the situation only aggravated the evil.   The attractions which the
government added to city life by its action
kept former residents in Rome and drew others
to the city.

Closely related to this question of the alarm-
ing growth of the larger cities was the displacement of the native stock in Rome and
Italy by people from abroad.   We have
already noticed that nearly ninety per cent.
of the permanent residents of Rome under the
Empire were of foreign extraction.   Rome was
therefore facing the same situation which dis-
turbs us.   It is true that most of the foreigners
living in Italy were slaves or the descendants of
slaves, as is the case with the negroes in this
country.   It was an instance of forced rather
than of voluntary immigration, but the result-

ant change in the character of the population is the same in both cases. Not only was the city of Rome dominated by foreigners, but at Beneventum, and Milan, and throughout the country districts of Italy the same condition prevailed. In still another respect the change in the character of the population of Italy reminds us of a corresponding change in our own population. Fifty years ago most of our immigrants came from western Europe. That tide of immigration has decreased and we regard with some alarm the arrival at our ports now of large numbers of people from eastern and southeastern Europe. They come from countries whose languages, and political and social ideas are very different from ours. They do not readily accept our traditions and institutions. This was exactly the situation in Italy under the Empire. By very interesting studies which Professor Frank [40] and others have made of the names found on tombstones and in the records of trade-guilds it appears that "the whole of Italy as well as the Romanized portions of Gaul and Spain were during the Empire dominated in blood by the East." The result was disastrous to Roman traditions and to Roman political life. In Professor Frank's opinion, the fact that, even as early as the time of the Gracchi, " reform through orderly compromise gave way to revolution through bloodshed is largely due to the displacement of real Italic peoples by men of Oriental, Punic and Iberian stock." At all events the presence of this large Oriental element in the population of the West helps us to understand the comparative willingness with which Rome accepted the principate in place of the republic. It helps us to understand the development of autocracy, the gradual adoption of Oriental titles and ceremonial at court, and the partial acceptance by the people of the Oriental theory of the Emperor's power.

IV. SOME FINAL REFLECTIONS

THE history of all institutions has a deep value and an abiding interest to all those who have the courage to work upon it. It presents in every branch a regularly developed series of causes and consequences, and abounds in examples of that continuity of life, the realization of which is necessary to give the reader a personal hold on the past and a right judgment of the present. For the roots of the present lie deep in the past; and nothing in the past is dead to the man who would learn how the present comes to be what it is." So Stubbs wrote on finishing his history of the *English Constitution* and on sending it out to the public. What he has said when thinking of the beginnings of constitutional government in England is true in a higher degree of the relations of modern political institutions to those of Rome. This is the case partly because we owe to Rome so much of our political philosophy and so much of our political system. It is true partly

because our indebtedness to Rome in the field
of politics has not been appreciated, and consequently we have failed to understand the
origin and nature of many of our institutions.
The failure to recognize the great debt which
we owe to her was a natural oversight. The
great gulf of the Middle Ages lies between
Roman times and our own day. Until the
trend of political thought and the development
of society during that period came to be better
understood, the close relation which medieval
political theory and practice bore to that of
the Romans and our dependence on the medieval were not seen. Until very recently
students of modern political institutions rarely
carried their investigations beyond the limits
of their respective countries, or at the most
they did not go back beyond the Renaissance.
But as the Carlyles have said in their *History
of Mediaeval Political Theory:* " From the
lawyers of the second century to the theorists
of the French Revolution, the history of political thought is continuous, changing in form,
modified in content, but still the same in its
fundamental conceptions." Many writers on
political science in ignorance or in disregard
of this continuity tell us, for instance, that the

representative principle was unknown in antiquity, or that the jury system was of English or Scandinavian origin. But fortunately a few scholars, like Bryce, who have an acquaintance with classical institutions, are gradually correcting these errors and helping us to see the way in which many of our modern political theories and institutions have come to us from Rome.

Our political indebtedness to the Romans takes two different forms. We have inherited many theories and institutions from them, and in the second place we have before us for our guidance their experience in dealing with difficult practical problems. As we have noticed in the preceding chapters, they have taught us to study actual governmental systems rather than to attempt the construction of Utopias. We owe to them the fruitful suggestion that the state may be compared to an organism. The conception of the brotherhood of man goes back to the early Empire, and out of this conception international law, and its counterpart, civil law, have developed. Roman writers recognized the three forms of government, monarchy, aristocracy, and democracy, and pointed out the importance of dividing the functions of government between the legislative, executive and judicial branches. From them we have derived our accepted doctrine of popular sovereignty, and to them the theory of the divine right of kings may be traced. The Romans developed the distinction which is so vital in English common law between statutes and customs, officially recognized, and showed the great advantages inherent in a flexible constitution which is made up of these two elements. They have handed down to us the representative principle, the jury method of trial, civil law, a clear conception of the rights of a citizen, a jealous regard for law and tradition, a comprehensive system of political checks and balances, model systems of local government and civil service, and methods of governing, civilizing, and unifying alien peoples which have never been equalled.

It was this final contribution that Rome made to civilization of which Mommsen was thinking, toward the end of his long study of Roman history and institutions, when he wrote: " If an angel of the Lord were to strike the balance whether the domain ruled by Severus Antoninus was governed with the greater intelligence and the greater humanity at that time or in the present day, whether civilization and national prosperity generally have since that time advanced or retrograded, it is very doubtful whether the decision would prove to be in favor of the present."

NOTES AND BIBLIOGRAPHY

NOTES

1. The arrangements which Rome made with the several cities of Sicily are outlined by Cicero in his oration *In Verrem*, III. 12–14.

2. The traditional story of the Decemvirate and its codification of the *Laws of the Twelve Tables* is told graphically by Livy, III. 32–54. Some of the extant fragments of these laws may be seen in F. D. Allen's *Remnants of Early Latin*, Boston, 1899, pp. 84–92.

3. On the activities of the censors, cf. Heitland, *The Roman Republic, passim*.

4. On the government of the provinces under the Republic one may read Arnold-Shuckburgh, C. III.

5. There is an interesting discussion of the motives and policy of C. Gracchus by W. W. Fowler in his *Roman Essays and Interpretations,* Oxford, 1920, pp. 99–110.

6. A brilliant analysis of the political policies of Pompey and Caesar may be found in E. Meyer's *Caesars Monarchie und das Principat des Pompejus*, Stuttgart, 1919.

7. On the legal basis of the principate of Augustus, see Abbott, *Roman Political Institutions*, pp. 267–273.

8. For the provinces under Augustus, see Arnold-Shuckburgh, chapter IV. For a list of them, cf. Sandys, pp. 401 ff.

9. Five municipal charters are given in an English translation by E. G. Hardy in his *Six Roman Laws and Three Spanish Charters*, Oxford, 1911–12.

10. The famous edict of Caracalla, to which reference is made in the *Code* of Justinian and elsewhere, may now be seen in no. 40 of the *Griechische Papyri im Museum des Oberhessischen Geschichtsverein zu Giessen*, E. Kornemann and P. M. Meyer, Leipzig, 1910.

11. For the bureaux of Hadrian and his successors, see Hirschfeld.

12. The most convenient edition of the *Code* of Justinian is to be found in the *Corpus Iuris Civilis,* 3 vols., ed. by Mommsen and others. Berlin, 1895.

13. The Latin text of the constitution of Vespasian may be found in K. E. Bruns, *Fontes Iuris Romani Antiqui,* Leipzig, 1893,[7] no. 56.

14. Cf. F. F. Abbott, on "The Referendum and the Recall Among the Ancient Romans," in *The Sewanee Review,* XXIII. 84–94 (1915).

15. For Professor Frank's discussion of these wars, see chapters V, VI, and XIII. Cf., also, Livy, XXI. 4. 1.

16. For the comparison of the Roman Senate and the Senate of the U. S. see the chapter on "The Story of Two Oligarchies."

17. For a fuller discussion of representative government among the Romans under the Republic, see Frank's *Roman Imperialism,* pp. 45, 209, 299, 301.

18. The oath of the Fascisti may be found in the *London Times* of Jan. 2, 1923. The best literature at present on the movement is *Discorsi Politici,* Benito Mussolini (Milan; *Essercizio Tipografico del "Popolo d'Italia,"* 1922). *Il Fascismo nella Vita Italiana,* Pietro Gorgolini. Preface by B. Mussolini (Turin; Anonima Libraria Italiana). *Fascismo Liberatore,* Cipriano Giachetti (Florence; Bemporad).

19. For the praetor's court see Abbott, *Roman Political Institutions,* pp. 105 ff.

20. A striking illustration of the looseness of procedure in Roman courts is given by Cicero in a letter to Atticus (*ad Atticum,* I. 16. 3–6), translated by E. O. Winstedt, *Letters to Atticus,* 3 vols., New York, 1919, in *The Loeb Classical Library.* On the course of a trial in a Roman court, cf. A. H. J. Greenidge, *The Legal Procedure of Cicero's Time,* Oxford, 1901, pp. 456–504.

21. On taxation in the provinces, see Arnold-Shuckburgh, chapter VI. On the customs duties, see R. L. V.

Cagnat, *Étude Historique sur les Impôts Indirects chez les Romains,* Paris, 1882.

22. On Diocletian's tax system, see Pauly-Wissowa-Kroll, III. 1513 ff.; Daremberg-Saglio, V. 434 ff.

23. "Rome's First Coinage," in *Classical Philology,* XIV. 314–327 (1919).

24. On life in the provinces see Bouchier's books cited in the Bibliography.

25. The road-systems in the provinces may be seen in Murray's *Small Classical Atlas,* or in H. S. Jones' *Companion to Roman History,* Oxford, 1912, map 4.

26. See Reid, pp. 279 ff.

27. See Chapters I and II in the *Common People of Ancient Rome.*

28. A detailed account of the method of founding Colonies and a list of them may be found in Pauly-Wissowa-Kroll, IV. 510 ff.

29. For an account of the Idaho Colony, see Albert Shaw, "From New York to Idaho," in *The American Review of Reviews,* LXIV. 177–182 (1921).

30. See the chapter on trade-guilds and corporations in Abbott's *Common People of Ancient Rome.*

30a. This statement does not apply to Asia Minor where we do know of industrial strikes in Roman times at Ephesus, Pergamum, Miletus, and Sardis. That of the bakers at Ephesus (Kern, *Die Inschriften von Magnesia,* no. 114, an inscription which we now know is from Ephesus) took place in the second century A.D. The other strikes are those of builders, one in the second century A.D. at Miletus on the Roman theatre (*Sitz. Berl. Ak.* 1904, p. 83); for Pergamum, cf. *Athen. Mitt.* XXIV, 1899, p. 199 (also second cent.); for Sardis *C.I.G.* 3647. An article by W. H. Buckler on *Labor Disputes in the Province of Asia* which will soon appear in *Anatolian Studies in Honor of Sir W. M. Ramsay,* Manchester, 1923, discusses this question. [D. M. R.]

31. On the failure of "big business" to determine the policy of the Roman state, see Frank's *Roman Imperialism.* For a different view, cf. Ferrero.

32. " Race Mixture In The Roman Empire," in *The American Historical Review,* XXI. 689–708 (1916).

33. Among the executives who have appealed directly to the voters may be mentioned Governor Hughes of New York State and Presidents Roosevelt and Wilson.

34. Augustus mentions his gratuities to soldiers in chapter 17 of his *Res Gestae Divi Augusti;* translated into English, *The Deeds of Augustus,* by W. Fairley, University of Pennsylvania, Philadelphia, 1898.

35. On methods of calculating the population of the city of Rome, see J. Beloch's *Bevölkerung der griechisch-römischen Welt*, Leipzig, 1886, chapter IX. sec. 2 and " Die Bevölkerung Italiens im Altertum," in *Klio,* III. 471–490 (1903).

36. On Diocletian's edict see the chapter on " Diocletian's Edict and the High Cost of Living " in Abbott's *Common People of Ancient Rome*

37. See the *Theodosian Code, (Theodosiani Libri XVI* ed. Th. Mommsen, Berlin, 1905), 10, 19, 1. 2. 8.

38. On compulsion to work in the mines, see the *Theodosian Code,* 10, 19, 5. 6. 7. and 15.

39. For Pliny's inquiries see the *Epistulae ad Traianum,* 39; cf. 31 on work in the mines.

40. For the influx into Italy and the West of men of Oriental extraction see T. Frank, in *The American Historical Review,* XXI. 689–708 (1916) and Frank's *Economic History of Rome,* pp. 154 ff. *et passim.*

BIBLIOGRAPHY

I. General Histories of Rome

BOAK, A. E. R., *A History of Rome to 565 A.D.* New York, 1921.

FERRERO, G., *The Greatness and Decline of Rome.* 5 vols. New York, 1909.

FOWLER, W. WARDE, *Rome* (Home University Library). London, 1912.

FRANK, T., *Roman Imperialism.* New York, 1914.

FRANK, T., *A History of Rome,* New York, 1923.

GIBBON, EDWARD, *The Decline and Fall of the Roman Empire* (Edition of J. B. Bury). 7 vols. London, 1896–1900.

HEITLAND, W. E., *The Roman Republic.* 3 vols. Cambridge, England, 1909.

MOMMSEN, TH., *The History of Rome* (Translated by W. P. Dickson). 5 vols. New York, 1895.

PELHAM, H. F., *Outlines of Roman History.* New York, 1905.[4]

JONES, H. STUART, *The Roman Empire, B.C. 29 — A.D. 476* (The Story of the Nations). New York, 1908.

SCHILLER, H., *Geschichte der römischen Kaiserzeit.* 2 vols. Gotha, 1883.

II. The Provinces and Municipalities

ARNOLD, W. T.,-SHUCKBURGH, E. S., *The Roman System of Provincial Administration.* Oxford and New York, 1914.

LIEBENAM, W., *Städteverwaltung im römischen Kaiserreiche.* Leipzig, 1900.

[175]

MARQUARDT, J., *Römische Staatsverwaltung*, vol. I. Leipzig, 1881.

MOMMSEN, TH., *The Provinces of the Roman Empire from Caesar to Diocletian* (Translation by W. P. Dickson). 2 vols. New York, 1909.

REID, J. S., *The Municipalities of the Roman Empire.* Cambridge, England, 1913.

III. POLITICAL INSTITUTIONS

ABBOTT, F. F., *A History and Description of Roman Political Institutions.* Boston, 1911.[3]

BOTSFORD, G. W., *The Roman Assemblies.* New York, 1909.

HIRSCHFIELD, O., *Die kaiserlichen Verwaltungsbeamten bis auf Diocletian.* Berlin, 1905.[2]

MOMMSEN, TH., *Römisches Staatsrecht.* 3 vols. Leipzig, 1887.

WILLEMS, P., *Le Droit Public Romain.* Louvain, 1888.[6]

WILLEMS, P., *Le Sénat de la République Romaine.* 3 vols. Louvain, 1883.

WILLOUGHBY, W. W., *The Political Theorics of the Ancient World.* New York, 1903.

IV. SOCIAL AND ECONOMIC LIFE

ABBOTT, F. F., *Society and Politics in Ancient Rome.* New York, 1909.

ABBOTT, F. F., *The Common People of Ancient Rome.* New York, 1911.

BOUCHIER, E. S., *Life and Letters in Roman Africa.* Oxford, 1913.

BOUCHIER, E. S., *Spain under the Roman Empire.* Oxford, 1914.

BOUCHIER, E. S., *Syria as a Roman Province.* Oxford, 1916.

BOUCHIER, E. S., *Sardinia in Ancient Times.* Oxford, 1917.

BIBLIOGRAPHY

DILL, S., *Roman Society from Nero to Marcus Aurelius.*
New York, 1905.

FOWLER, W. W., *Social Life at Rome in the Age of Cicero.*
New York, 1909.

FRANK, T., *An Economic History of Rome.* Baltimore,
1920.

FRIEDLÄNDER, L., *Roman Life and Manners under the
Early Empire* (Translation by Freese and Magnus).
4 vols. London and New York, 1908–1913.

V. GENERAL HANDBOOKS

DAREMBERG, CHARLES, ET SAGLIO, M. E., *Dictionnaire des
Antiquités Grecques et Romaines.* 5 vols. Paris,
1875–1919.

JONES, H. STUART, *Companion to Roman History.*
Oxford, 1912.

LÜBKER, F., *Reallexikon des klassischen Altertums.*
Leipzig, 1914.[8]

PAULY, A. F. VON, WISSOWA, GEORG, KROLL, W., *Real-
Encyclopaedie der classischen Altertumswissenschaft.*
11 vols. (incomplete). Stuttgart, 1894–1922.

SANDYS, J. E., *A Companion to Latin Studies.* Cambridge, England, 1921.[3]

Our Debt to Greece and Rome

AUTHORS AND TITLES

AUTHORS AND TITLES

Homer. *John A. Scott.*

Sappho. *David M. Robinson.*

Euripides. *F. L. Lucas.*

Aristophanes. *Louis E. Lord.*

Demosthenes. *Charles D. Adams.*

The Poetics of Aristotle. *Lane Cooper.*

Greek Rhetoric and Literary Criticism. *W. Rhys Roberts.*

Lucian. *Francis G. Allinson.*

Cicero and His Influence. *John C. Rolfe.*

Catullus. *Karl P. Harrington.*

Lucretius and His Influence. *George Depue Hadzsits.*

Ovid. *Edward Kennard Rand.*

Horace. *Grant Showerman.*

Virgil. *John William Mackail.*

Seneca The Philosopher. *Richard Mott Gummere.*

Apuleius. *Elizabeth Hazelton Haight.*

Martial. *Paul Nixon.*

Platonism. *Alfred Edward Taylor.*

Aristotelianism. *John L. Stocks.*

Stoicism. *Robert Mark Wenley.*

Language and Philology. *Roland G. Kent.*

AUTHORS AND TITLES

AESCHYLUS AND SOPHOCLES. *J. T. Sheppard.*

GREEK RELIGION. *Walter Woodburn Hyde.*

SURVIVALS OF ROMAN RELIGION. *Gordon J. Laing.*

MYTHOLOGY. *Jane Ellen Harrison.*

ANCIENT BELIEFS IN THE IMMORTALITY OF THE SOUL. *Clifford H. Moore.*

STAGE ANTIQUITIES. *James Turney Allen.*

PLAUTUS AND TERENCE. *Gilbert Norwood.*

ROMAN POLITICS. *Frank Frost Abbott.*

PSYCHOLOGY, ANCIENT AND MODERN. *G. S. Brett.*

ANCIENT AND MODERN ROME. *Rodolfo Lanciani.*

WARFARE BY LAND AND SEA. *Eugene S. McCartney.*

THE GREEK FATHERS. *James Marshall Campbell.*

GREEK BIOLOGY AND MEDICINE. *Henry Osborn Taylor.*

MATHEMATICS. *David Eugene Smith.*

LOVE OF NATURE AMONG THE GREEKS AND ROMANS. *H. R. Fairclough.*

ANCIENT WRITING AND ITS INFLUENCE. *B. L. Ullman.*

GREEK ART. *Arthur Fairbanks.*

ARCHITECTURE. *Alfred M. Brooks.*

ENGINEERING. *Alexander P. Gest.*

MODERN TRAITS IN OLD GREEK LIFE. *Charles Burton Gulick.*

ROMAN PRIVATE LIFE. *Walton Brooks McDaniel.*

GREEK AND ROMAN FOLKLORE. *William Reginald Halliday.*

ANCIENT EDUCATION. *J. F. Dobson.*